THE
SECOND BOOK
OF THE
TAO

BY STEPHEN MITCHELL

POETRY
Parables and Portraits

FICTION
The Frog Prince
Meetings with the Archangel

NONFICTION
A Thousand Names for Joy (with Byron Katie)
Loving What Is (with Byron Katie)
The Gospel According to Jesus

TRANSLATIONS AND ADAPTATIONS
The Second Book of the Tao
Gilgamesh
Bhagavad Gita
Real Power: Business Lessons from the Tao Te Ching (with James A. Autry)
Full Woman, Fleshly Apple, Hot Moon: Selected Poems of Pablo Neruda
Genesis
Ahead of All Parting: The Selected Poetry and Prose of Rainer Maria Rilke
A Book of Psalms
The Selected Poetry of Dan Pagis
Tao Te Ching
The Book of Job
The Selected Poetry of Yehuda Amichai (with Chana Bloch)
The Sonnets to Orpheus

The Lay of the Love and Death of Cornet Christoph Rilke
Letters to a Young Poet
The Notebooks of Malte Laurids Brigge
The Selected Poetry of Rainer Maria Rilke

EDITED BY STEPHEN MITCHELL

Question Your Thinking, Change the World: Quotations from Byron Katie
The Essence of Wisdom: Words from the Masters to Illuminate the Spiritual Path
Bestiary: An Anthology of Poems about Animals
Song of Myself
Into the Garden: A Wedding Anthology (with Robert Hass)
The Enlightened Mind: An Anthology of Sacred Prose
The Enlightened Heart: An Anthology of Sacred Poetry
Dropping Ashes on the Buddha: The Teaching of Zen Master Seung Sahn

THE
SECOND BOOK
OF THE
TAO

Compiled and adapted from the
Chuang-tzu and the Chung Yung,
with commentaries

STEPHEN MITCHELL

THE PENGUIN PRESS

New York

2009

THE PENGUIN PRESS
Published by the Penguin Group
Penguin Group (USA) Inc., 375 Hudson Street, • New York, New York 10014, U.S.A. •
Penguin Group (Canada), 90 Eglinton Avenue East, Suite 700, Toronto, Ontario, Canada M4P 2Y3
(a division of Pearson Penguin Canada Inc.) • Penguin Books Ltd, 80 Strand, London WC2R 0RL,
England • Penguin Ireland, 25 St. Stephen's Green, Dublin 2, Ireland (a division of Penguin Books Ltd) •
Penguin Books Australia Ltd, 250 Camberwell Road, Camberwell, Victoria 3124, Australia
(a division of Pearson Australia Group Pty Ltd) • Penguin Books India Pvt Ltd, 11 Community Centre,
Panchsheel Park, New Delhi—110 017, India • Penguin Group (NZ), 67 Apollo Drive, Rosedale,
North Shore 0632, New Zealand (a division of Pearson New Zealand Ltd) • Penguin Books
(South Africa) (Pty) Ltd, 24 Sturdee Avenue, Rosebank, Johannesburg 2196, South Africa

Penguin Books Ltd, Registered Offices:
80 Strand, London WC2R 0RL, England

First published in 2009 by The Penguin Press,
a member of Penguin Group (USA) Inc.

1   3   5   7   9   10   8   6   4   2

Copyright © Stephen Mitchell, 2009
All rights reserved

Some of the selections from the Chung Yung first appeared, in different form, in
The Enlightened Mind: An Anthology of Sacred Prose, edited by Stephen Mitchell, HarperCollins, 1991.
Selections from Seng-ts'an's "The Mind of Absolute Trust," *The Enlightened Heart:
An Anthology of Sacred Poetry*, edited by Stephen Mitchell, HarperCollins, 1989.
Selections from *I Need Your Love—Is That True?* by Byron Katie with Michael Katz, Harmony, 2005,
and *A Thousand Names for Joy* by Byron Katie with Stephen Mitchell, Harmony, 2007.
Selections from *The Complete Works of Chuang Tzu*, translated by Burton Watson. Copyright © 1968
Columbia University Press. Reprinted by permission of the publisher.

LIBRARY OF CONGRESS CATALOGING IN PUBLICATION DATA

Mitchell, Stephen.
The second book of the Tao : compiled and adapted from the Chuang-tzu and the
Chung Yung, with commentaries / Stephen Mitchell.
p. cm.
Includes bibliographical references.
ISBN 978-1-59420-203-2
1. Zhuangzi. Nanhua jing.   2. Zhong yong.   I. Zhuangzi. Nanhua jing. English. Selections.
II. Zhong yong. English. Selections.   III. Title.
BL1900.C576M57 2009
299.5'1482—dc22

2008034887
Printed in the United States of America

Book designed by Claire Naylon Vaccaro

To Katie:

always

CONTENTS

FOREWORD

"A second book of the Tao? There's no such thing! What did you do—pull it out of your hat?"

Well, yes, if *hat* is defined as the treasury of recorded wisdom that is our common birthright. In that treasury, there is nothing more precious than the wisdom of the ancient Chinese.

The selections in this book have been adapted from two Chinese anthologies that were probably compiled between 300 and 100 BCE: the Chuang-tzu, parts of which were written by the eponymous sage, Master Chuang (c. 369–c. 286 BCE), and the Chung Yung ("The Central Harmony"), which was ascribed to Confucius' grandson, Tzu-ssu (c. 483–c. 402 BCE). I have anthologized these anthologies, picking from them the freshest, clearest, most profound passages. Facing each chapter there is a brief commentary, which is meant to clarify the text or to complement it. I have written these in the spirit of Chuang-tzu, for whom nothing, thank goodness, was sacred.

The first book of the Tao (written by the perhaps legendary Lao-tzu) is the Tao Te Ching, that marvel of lucidity and grace, the classic manual on the art of living. What I wanted to create here was a left to its right, a yang to its yin, a companion volume and anti-manual. The Chuang-tzu had the perfect material for that: deep, subtle, with an audacity that can make your hair stand on end. If Lao-tzu is a smile, Chuang-tzu is a belly-laugh. He's the clown of the Absolute, the apotheosis of incredulity, Coyote among the bodhisattvas. And the Chung Yung provided a psychological and moral acuity of comparable depth.

Readers who are familiar with the Tao Te Ching but don't yet know the Chuang-tzu or the Chung Yung—or who, having dipped into them, were discouraged by their unevenness—are in for a treat. Naturally, since all three texts tell of the Tao that can't be told, there are passages in *The Second Book of the Tao* that overlap with the Tao Te Ching. But even these passages may strike you as revelations, as if some explorer had discovered a trove of unknown Lao-tzu scrolls buried in a desert cave. And there is much that will be entirely new: meditations on dreams, death, language, the I and the other, doing and not-doing, the origin of the universe, the absolute relativity of things.

In addition to these descriptions, we meet a cast of vivid characters, most of them humble artisans or servants, who show us what it means to be in harmony with the way things are: the monkey trainer who turns on a dime in his hilarious, compassionate diplomacy; Ting, Prince Wen-hui's cook, whose one-pointedness elevates butchering to the level of the performing arts and beyond; Pien the wheelwright, willing to risk his life to teach a ferocious nobleman that what is most valuable can't be taught; Ch'ing the woodworker, whose bell stand is so beautiful that people think a god must have made it; and Chi Hsing-tzu, trainer of champion gamecocks and virtuoso of patience. We also meet philosophers and fools: Lieh-tzu, who has an intimate chat with a skull; Hui-tzu, the epitome of logic and propriety, Chuang-tzu's friend and rival, straight man and foil; the ludicrous Marquis of Lu, who shows that the Golden Rule can be mere projected egotism; and Master Yu, who, even when afflicted with a grotesque deformity, never loses his cheerfulness and sense of gratitude. Finally there is Chuang-tzu himself. We meet him in a few delectable stories and dialogues, as he wakes up (maybe) from the dream of a butterfly, refuses the post of prime minister, celebrates the death of his beloved wife, or discusses the usefulness of the useless and the happiness of fish.

Chuang-tzu has been called a mystical anarchist, and it's true that his words sometimes have a contrarian flavor that seems to put them at odds with Lao-tzu's concern for enlightened government. Given the least semblance of control, Chuang-tzu offers a whole world of irreverence and subversion. But if you look more closely, you'll see that he is neither a mystic nor an anarchist. He's simply someone who doesn't linger in any mental construct about reality, someone who lives as effortless action and peace of heart, because he has freed himself from his own beliefs. What he subverts is conventional thinking, with its hierarchies of judgment, its *for*s and *against*s, *better*s and *worse*s, *inside*s and *outside*s, and its delusion that life is random, unfair, and somehow not good enough. Learn how to govern your own mind, Chuang-tzu says, and the universe will govern itself. In this he is in wholehearted agreement with Lao-tzu and with the meticulous Tzu-ssu, for whom attention to the innermost self is the direct path to a just society.

One of the qualities I most treasure in Chuang-tzu is his sense of the spontaneous, the uncapturable. This makes it easy to follow in his footsteps. Since there are no footsteps, all you can follow is what he himself followed: the Tao. He had confidence that in being true to his own insight he was being true to his teacher Lao-tzu. There was nothing to say and no way to say it, yet it had to be said. As a Zen poet-descendant of his wrote more than a thousand years later,

The moon floats above the pine trees
as you sit on the veranda in the cool evening air.
Your fingertips move lightly along the flute.
The melody is so lovely that it makes the listeners weep.
But wisdom's flute has no holes
and its ancient clear music is beyond emotion.
Don't even try to play it
unless you can make the great sound of Lao-tzu.

What could be more useless than a flute with no holes? Yet, if you understand, you put it to your lips and the ancient clear music happens by itself. Had Chuang-tzu believed that there was anything to live up to, he would have been too intimidated even to try. There was nothing to live up to. There was only a passion for the genuine, a fascination with words, and a constant awareness that the ancient Masters are alive and well in the mind that doesn't know a thing.

ABOUT THE ADAPTATION

The texts on the left-hand pages of this book are not translations; they are adaptations, sometimes very free ones. Since I don't know Chinese, I have been entirely indebted to the work of three generations of scholars and translators. For the Chuang-tzu, Burton Watson's translation was the most helpful for my purposes, but I also studied the complete translations by Victor H. Mair, Martin Palmer, and Richard Wilhelm, the partial ones by A. C. Graham, Sam Hamill and J. P. Seaton, and David Hinton, and Thomas Merton's free version. For the Chung Yung, I have used the translations by Ku Hungming, Andrew Plaks, and Ezra Pound.

"Chuang-tzu is not only a remarkable philosopher," Octavio Paz said, "but also a great poet." Though the Chuang-tzu and the Chung Yung are written in prose, forty-nine of my chapters are in verse, because it quickly became apparent that verse would allow me to write a more lyrical and epigrammatic English. I have been particularly free with these chapters, and have sometimes expanded, contracted, paraphrased, improvised, changed images, changed meanings, so that I could create a music in English that seemed genuine to my inner ear.

With thirteen of the prose chapters I have been closer to the original text, though even with them my sentences occasionally wandered off in their own directions. (Two prose chapters—27 and 31—are free variations on the original themes by Chuang-tzu.) In the Notes on the Adaptation, I have appended a number of more literally translated passages for comparison.

As with my version of the Tao Te Ching, the chapters that describe the Master alternate between "she" and "he." In Chinese, the personal pronoun is gender-neutral; in English we have to choose. Since we are all, potentially, the Master—since the Master is, essentially, us—it seemed absurd and disrespectful to present the reader with a male archetype.

My original intention was to create a book of eighty-one chapters, like the Tao Te Ching. But after much searching and sifting, I couldn't find eighty-one passages of the highest quality. So instead of 81 (9^2 or 3^4) I settled on 64 (8^2 or 4^3) chapters. In this way, the number wasn't altogether arbitrary; and while 81 has a particular elegance to it, so does 64. Besides its arcane mathematical properties, it is the number of hexagrams in the I Ching, the number of squares on a chessboard, the number of sexual positions in the Kama Sutra, and the only two-digit number ever to star in a Beatles song.

THE
SECOND BOOK
OF THE
TAO

1

What is bestowed on us at birth
is called human nature.
The fulfillment of human nature
is called the Tao.
The cultivation of the Tao
is the deepest form of learning.

The Tao is the way things are,
which you can't depart from
even for one instant.
If you could depart from it,
it wouldn't be the Tao.
Therefore the Master
looks into her own heart
and respects what is unseen and unheard.

Nothing is more manifest than the hidden;
nothing is more obvious than the unseen.
Therefore the Master
pays attention to what is happening
within her innermost self.

We think that we know what human nature is, but what if our most cherished assumptions are wrong? What if all suffering is the result of confused thoughts? That would change our paradigm a bit.

We're born into the open, into the vast mind empty of meaning. Beyond thought, beyond things, reality just is. Human nature doesn't need to be fulfilled, nor do we need to cultivate what is already perfect. Once we recognize this, we return to the origin of all things. There is never a movement toward or away. We remain where we have always been, but now we know it, as if for the first time.

Departing from the Tao can happen only in the mind; it's an illusion that becomes our reality. Though we actually live in what is, we think ourselves into what isn't. Though every apparent detour *is* the path, we get lost in our imagined wanderings. That's why, if we're interested in freedom, there is nothing sweeter than to cultivate, cultivate: to get down, with trowel and hoe, into the thought-rich soil of the mind.

It's all about paying attention to what is happening within our innermost self, until the unseen, the unquestioned, is as obvious as the seen. When the mind is free of its thoughts, it becomes its own fulfillment.

2

Before sorrow, anger,
longing, or fear have arisen,
you are in the center.
When these emotions appear
and you know how to see through them,
you are in harmony.
That center is the root of the universe;
that harmony is the Tao,
which reaches out to all things.

Once you find the center
and achieve harmony,
heaven and earth take their proper places
and all things are fully nourished.

COMMENTARY

This chapter is about saving the world. You save the world when you save yourself. (There's no one else you *can* save.) Returning to the center is thus an act of infinite kindness.

There's nothing wrong with sorrow, anger, longing, or fear; a painful emotion is just a signal that you've left the center. When you are at peace, everything is at peace. What seemed like cacophony becomes the music of the spheres: a suite for unaccompanied mind.

Living in harmony with the way things are, the mind finds its center everywhere, its circumference nowhere. The part becomes the whole; what is becomes what should be. Heaven takes its proper, its *only* place: on earth.

3

The great Tao cannot be named,
great discernment cannot be seen,
great benevolence is not gentle,
great modesty is not meek,
great courage is not aggressive.

When you truly understand
the Tao that cannot be named,
you become rooted in not-knowing.
This is called "inner radiance."
Add to it, it is never full;
take from it, it is never depleted.
Who can tell where it comes from?
It is the inexhaustible treasury.

COMMENTARY

Who named it "the Tao" in the first place? I would like to talk to that fellow. I'd like to give him a piece of my mind. The Tao. The Way. Imagine: naming the unnamable! This may have seemed like a clever idea at the time, but it led to endless complications. Before long, people were searching everywhere for the Way. Intellectuals began to wear themselves out debating whether it existed or not, or whether perhaps it both existed and didn't exist, or whether indeed it neither existed nor didn't exist. Scholars wrote tomes, with characters brushed in the blackest of ink, to prove that the Way goes this way or that. Moralists determined what is on the Way and what is off, discerning, down to the minutest particulars, exactly what we must do never to stray from the Way. Thus Taoism was born. But every ism is a wasm. It's already old news: an exoskeleton from which the living truth has moved on.

The Tao that cannot be named is the intelligence of the universe: whatever is happening right now. The mind that realizes this is the don't-know mind, which is open to all possibilities because it doesn't believe its own thoughts. What more is there to say? Except that there's a radiance about people who have settled into the depths of not-knowing. You can see it in their eyes. It doesn't depend on what happens or doesn't happen. They have found the inexhaustible treasure, in the most obvious place of all.

4

When we exhaust our minds by clinging to a particular side of reality without realizing the underlying oneness, it's called "three in the morning." What does that mean?

A monkey trainer, handing out acorns, said, "Each of you will get three in the morning and four in the afternoon." The monkeys were outraged.

So he said, "All right, then: you'll get four in the morning and three in the afternoon." The monkeys were delighted.

Nothing essential had changed, yet one statement produced anger, and the other, joy. The trainer simply knew how to adapt to reality, and he lost nothing by it.

Thus the Master uses his skill to harmonize with both sides, and rests in the Tao, which makes all things equal. This is called "walking on two paths at once."

COMMENTARY

The whole human condition is present in this tricky little tale, which would be sad if it weren't so ridiculous. Although from the standpoint of the monkeys it's about the power of righteous indignation, from the standpoint of the monkey trainer, behind the scenes, it's about skillful management. You have to admire his one-two punch; he's both bad cop and good cop. But what is the trainer training the monkeys in, anyway? Discernment? If so, he's being made a monkey of.

Whenever we cling to a particular side of reality, it's we who are the monkeys, losing ourselves in outrage or partial delight. If we look more carefully, though, we can see that reality has only one side, like a Möbius strip. Stars or raindrops, acorns or ashes, apparent blessings, apparent disasters—when the mind is clear, each is an occasion for rejoicing. That's what discernment is about.

Once our mind-monkeys are fully trained, it's all good. In the mathematics of mental peace, three equals four, one equals zero. Adapting to reality means recognizing that nothing underlies or overlays it. The Master can travel on two paths at once, like a photon, because his mind is free. He's subatomic and supererogatory. He knows that all ways are the Way and that ultimately he is neither coming nor going.

5

The ancient Masters saw deeply.
How deep was their insight?
They realized that nothing exists.
This is perfect understanding.

Those at the next stage
thought that things existed
but saw no boundaries between them.

Next came those who saw boundaries
but didn't judge things as good or bad.

When judgments arose,
understanding was damaged;
when understanding was damaged,
preferences became ingrained.

But is there really such a thing
as damage or wholeness?
The Master understands
that there is nothing to understand.

COMMENTARY

The ancient Masters saw deeply indeed. They realized that since nothing lasts longer than the untraceable instant, nothing ultimately exists. They also realized that "nothing" is something, and that the opposite of a profound truth is another profound truth. Nothing exists. Something exists. "All Cretans are liars," said the Cretan. It's better to keep your mouth shut.

Still, these old fellows were on to something. If nothing exists as we know it, if time and space are intellectual categories, there's nothing we can actually grasp, to arrange or disarrange. This leaves us free. It leaves us at play in the cosmic theater of the mind. All the world's a stage, and we are the non-actors. Can life be as simple as that?

It went downhill from there, to the next stage, then the next. Boundaries! Preferences!! Attachments!!! And before we knew it, our days filled up with screaming babies, mortgage payments, nasty messages in the mailbox.

Damage and wholeness are in the eyes of the beholder, of course. If you're a child, there's nothing more fun than going downhill. A tragedy is a comedy misunderstood. Once you realize what you are, there's nothing left but gratitude and laughter.

6

Everything can be seen as a this;
everything can be seen as a that.
The that depends on the this;
the this mirrors the that.
One follows from the other;
each is inseparable from both.
You can't have right without wrong,
life without death,
the true without the false.

The Master is not trapped in opposites.
His this is also a that.
He sees that life becomes death
and death becomes life, that right
has a kernel of wrong within it
and wrong a kernel of right,
that the true turns into the false
and the false into the true.
He understands that nothing is absolute,
that since every point of view
depends on the viewer,
affirmation and denial
are equally beside the point.

The place where the this and the that
are not opposed to each other
is called "the pivot of the Tao."
When we find this pivot, we find ourselves
at the center of the circle,
and here we sit, serene,
while Yes and No keep chasing each other
around the circumference, endlessly.

Mind can only create the qualities of good and bad by comparing. Remove the comparison, and there go the qualities. What remains is the pure unknown: ungraspable object, ungraspable subject, and the clear light of awareness streaming through.

The pivot of the Tao is the mind free of its thoughts. It doesn't believe that this is a this or that that is a that. Let Yes and No sprint around the circumference toward a finish line that doesn't exist. How can they stop trying to win the argument of life until *you* stop? When you do, you realize that you were the only one running. Yes was you, No was you, the whole circumference, with its colored banners, its pom-pom girls and frenzied crowds—that was you as well.

At the center, the eyes open and again it's the sweet morning of the world. There's nothing here to limit you, no one here to draw a circumference. In fact, there's no one here—not even you.

7

Nothing in the world is bigger
than the tip of an autumn hair,
and Mount Everest is tiny.
No one in the world has lived longer
than a stillborn child,
and Methuselah died young.
The universe came into being
the moment that I was born,
and all things are one with me.

Since all things are one,
how can I put that into words?
But since I just said they are one,
how can my words mean nothing?
The one plus my words make two,
and the two plus the one make three.
If we continue in this way,
even the greatest mathematician
couldn't calculate where it will end.
If by moving from non-being to being
we get to three, what happens
when we move from being to being?

It's better just to leave things alone.

COMMENTARY

There are paradoxes born of wit and paradoxes born of insight. No thought is true, but some thoughts are so much truer than the ones we're used to that they seem absurd at first glance. It's all a question of perspective.

Down at the level of the micro, there *is* no macro. If you get small enough, you see that the world isn't solid and that uncertainty is the only thing that's certain, perhaps. Thus, everything the electron meets is electronal. Ditto a galaxy: its consciousness, if it has one, is as little aware of a planet as you are of a corpuscle. We can't stand outside the system and point to what's real, because what's real is defined by the system. This is relativity writ large. The fastest thing in the universe isn't light: it's mind.

All things may be one with me, but am I one with them? That's the issue. And once I am one, what then? Even the one is excessive for anyone who wants to be meticulous. Look where it leads, after all—to two, to three, to infinity, to an infinity of infinities and beyond: always the unattainable, unassuageable *beyond*.

Of course, the nothing is out of the question as well, since there's already a word for it. Not one? Not nothing? This leaves you in an ideal position: speechless, delighted, and ready to say the most nonsensical things, if only they make sense.

8

How do I know that loving life
isn't simply a delusion?
How do I know
that when we're afraid of death
we aren't like someone
who left home as a young child
and has forgotten the way back?
How do I know that the dead
aren't so happy that they wonder
why they once clung to life?

You may dream that you're at a banquet
and wake up to find yourself miserable.
You may dream that you're sobbing your heart out
and wake up to find yourself at ease.
How, in the middle of a dream,
can you know that you're actually dreaming?
In the middle of a dream, you may even
try to interpret the dream;
only after you wake up
do you realize that you were dreaming.
Someday there will be
a great awakening, when we know
that all this was one big dream.

And when I say that we're dreaming,
of course I am dreaming too.

COMMENTARY

How do I *know*? Well, I don't. So that settles that.

But loving life isn't a problem. Preferring life to death: that's what causes the confusion.

It could be (if there were such a thing as departing) that death is the return to a presence the wandering mind has long forgotten. It could be (if there were such a thing as separate beings) that the dead look upon our attachment to life like fond grandparents watching a teenager's first tumultuous love affair. It could be, in fact, that the dead are nothing but their own delight, there (if there were such a thing as space) where they know even as they are known.

We are close to waking up when we dream that we are dreaming. All the imagined ups and downs, the hubbub and reversals of fortune, are what most people call life. But before and after, at the point where the end meets its beginning, there is only what has woken up from the cycle of waking, dreaming, and dreamless sleep.

As for a "great awakening": dream on. When do you think that that *someday* will come, after all? Isn't it enough just to open your eyes, feel the pillow beneath your head, and see the hands of the alarm clock pointing to this very moment (as if there were such a thing as time)?

9

Chuang-tzu dreamt that he was a butterfly, fluttering here and there, carefree, unaware of a Chuang-tzu. Then he woke up, and there he was again: Chuang-tzu, beyond a doubt. But was he Chuang-tzu who had dreamt that he was a butterfly, or a butterfly now dreaming that he was Chuang-tzu? There must be *some* difference between Chuang-tzu and a butterfly! This is called "the transformation of things."

COMMENTARY

The most famous dream in human history. You may feel that, as with Zeno's paradoxes, there is something specious going on here, if only you could put your finger on it. But the more closely you examine the story, the more penetrating Chuang-tzu's question becomes. He's the anti-serpent in the garden, tempting you to take one little bite from the Tree of Life. He's Alice's Caterpillar, puffing on his hookah and asking, "Who are *you*?" In fact, with time running backward as in a Feynman diagram, Alice's Caterpillar could well have metamorphosed into Chuang-tzu's butterfly, just to prove a point.

You may be recalling that *psychē*, the Greek word for "soul," can also mean "butterfly." But let's leave the Greeks out of this. Chuang-tzu is definitely Chinese, he thinks. His butterfly is not a metamorphosis, not a metaphor; it's just a butterfly. Just? How can we know what depths of joy lie hidden within that pinpoint of a brain? The whole world contained in a garden, in a single flower! All time contained in a summer's day, and life one all-embracing multiorgasmic fragrance!

And who knows what a butterfly might dream of? Of an ancient Chinese philosopher, perhaps, or of a nineteenth-century Oxford don who was enchanted by little girls. This particular butterfly woke up as Chuang-tzu—or was it Chuang-tzu who woke up as himself? "There he was again, beyond a doubt." Beyond a doubt? Ha!

Things change before our very eyes, whether our eyes are open or shut. A butterfly becomes a man, a man becomes a question mark, a question mark becomes a winged creature, carefree, doing whatever it likes. Thus identity melts away, and we are left with something more valuable: a self—a non-self—that includes it all.

10

There was a beginning of time.
There was a time before the beginning
of time. There was a time
before the time before
the beginning of time. There is being.
If there is being, there must be
non-being. If there is non-being,
there must have been a time when even
non-being didn't exist.
Suddenly there was non-being.
But can non-being really exist,
and can being not-exist?

I just said something.
But did what I just said really
say anything, or not?

COMMENTARY

The mind loves to play its little games about time. It visualizes time as space, it fills in the blanks, it sees a before and an after, it befores the before, afters the after, befores the after, afters the before—and that's just the beginning. By the time it has finished articulating futures and pasts, it is bound up in its own complications, a ball of perplexity, waiting for the coup de grâce.

How thorough Chuang-tzu is in deconstructing himself! He delights in being hoist with his own petard; he's like the cartoon character sitting out on a limb, backward, and sawing it away—except that he knows perfectly well what will happen. His questions are more than Socratic. They cut to the bone.

Here's the open secret: There is no beginning of time, only a beginning of thought. It arises from the I, the subtlest thought of all, which splits reality down the middle, creating this and that, inner and outer, and all the other mirrored 0's and 1's that make up this apparent universe. Then, suddenly, one fine day, mind realizes that it knows nothing, that it *is* nothing, and sets itself free. Being? Non-being? Give me a break.

11

The Master doesn't aim for success,
doesn't avoid failure,
doesn't act with a motive,
doesn't try to follow the Tao.
She speaks when she is silent,
says nothing when she speaks,
and remains pure
amid the world's dust and grime.

The Master soars past the sun and moon,
tucks the universe under her arm,
and is one with the ten thousand things.
She lets the confused stay confused
if that is what they want
and is always available
to those with a passion for the truth.
In the welter of opinions,
she is content with not-knowing.
She makes distinctions
but doesn't take them seriously.
She sees the world constantly breaking
apart, and stays centered in the whole.
She sees the world endlessly changing
and never wants it to be
different from what it is.

COMMENTARY

There's nothing special about the Master. She doesn't know any secrets, and she doesn't live in some state of exalted consciousness. She's just like you, except that she no longer believes her own thoughts. "When I attained unexcelled perfect enlightenment," the Buddha said, "there was nothing that I attained."

The mind at peace with itself needs only what it has, wants only what it is.

12

The Tao penetrates
into every last corner of the universe.
Because it is deep and wide
and extends its power everywhere,
it transcends all things.
Because it transcends all things,
it is at the heart of all things.
It shows itself without being seen,
creates without doing,
fulfills without an intention.
It obeys only its own law;
thus its creations are infinite.
In this it is like heaven and earth.
Heaven is a bright emptiness,
but in its measureless extent
it contains the sun, moon, planets,
and the uncountable stars,
and through it all things are illumined.
Earth is a heap of soil,
but in its width and depth
it holds up the great mountains,
the rivers, lakes, and seas,
trees, plants, animals, birds,
fish, and the monsters of the deep:
all life in its manifold splendor.

The Tao claims nothing for itself;
thus it contains all things.

COMMENTARY

We love the nature of things, even when we don't understand it. Who doesn't take pleasure in light, so married to vision before any eyes existed? Who doesn't think that light is beautiful, whatever it happens to shine on? We're instinctively attracted to what is all-embracing and all-allowing. We can oppose it only if we construe it as something it's not.

The nature of things can't help but be our own nature as well. What we love in the world is what we discover in ourselves. The infinite inclusiveness of heaven, the unshakable support of earth: how could we notice them if they weren't qualities of our noticing mind? Whatever the self describes, describes the self.

13

Things are the way they are
because we think they're that way.
Good or bad,
acceptable or unacceptable,
they conform to the way we see them.
Originally, in themselves,
all things are good and acceptable.

That is why all things—a blade
of grass or a hundred-foot pine,
a leper or a legendary beauty,
a national hero or a traitor—
are equal in the Tao.
None is more important
or more valued than any other.
Their difference is their completeness.
Only the person of true vision
can recognize them as equal.
He sees past his own judgments,
doesn't think *more* or *less*,
and accepts without even trying to.
This is called "honoring the Tao."

"There is nothing either good or bad but thinking makes it so." This one liberating truth can be said in a hundred ways. Each goes to the root of the matter.

What happens when we realize that the world appears according to our perception of it? For one thing, we don't take our judgments so seriously. The judging I begins to unravel. Eventually, we discover that everything exists in itself, beyond comparison, beyond judgments, as it did for God on the evening of the sixth day: "Behold, it is very good."

When we look at creatures from this point of vision, it's easy to see that a blade of grass is as important as a pine tree, a minnow as valued as a whale. Size and complexity have nothing to do with it. Evolution doesn't mean progress. Which is more conscious, the butterfly or the flower?

The Master sees that we're all doing the best we can with what we've been given. Realizing this, he doesn't expect anything of anyone. Thus, as he honors himself, he naturally honors the Tao.

14

Prince Wen-hui's cook, Ting, was cutting up an ox. Every touch of his hand, every ripple of his shoulders, every step of his feet, every thrust of his knees, every cut of his knife, was in perfect harmony, like the dance of the Mulberry Grove, like the chords of the Lynx Head music.

"Well done!" said the prince. "How did you gain such skill?"

Putting down his knife, Ting said, "I follow the Tao, Your Highness, which goes beyond all skills. When I first began cutting up oxen, all I could see was the ox. After three years, I had learned to look beyond the ox. Nowadays I see with my whole being, not with my eyes. I sense the natural lines, and my knife slides through by itself, never touching a joint, much less a bone.

"A good cook changes knives once a year: he cuts. An ordinary cook changes knives once a month: he hacks. This knife of mine has lasted for nineteen years; it has cut up thousands of oxen, but its blade is as sharp as if it were new. Between the joints there are spaces, and the blade has no thickness. Having no thickness, it slips right through; there's more than enough room for it. And when I come to a difficult part, I slow down, I focus my attention, I barely move, the knife finds its way, until suddenly the flesh falls apart on its own. I stand there and let the joy of the work fill me. Then I wipe the blade clean and put it away."

"Bravo!" cried the prince. "From the words of this cook, I have learned how to live my life."

In his rules for right livelihood, the Buddha proscribed trafficking in meat (and in weapons, slaves, intoxicants, and poison). Clearly, he never imagined someone like Prince Wen-hui's cook: an artist of ox flesh, a saint of the bloody carcass. So much for rules. This just shows that nothing in life can be categorized or excluded. The whole world is our palette.

Ting, it must be said, was a man of supreme integrity, who trusted what is and needed no one's appreciation. For decades he had been putting on his one-man show for an audience of zero: no one was watching—not even he. The glorious harmony of motion and intention simply happened without him. How can we know the dancer from the dance?

In the practice of butchery, he had learned how to step aside and let his body do the thinking. He followed the Tao into a world of unadulterated sensation, an Eden of the don't-know mind. The vast universe, with its myriad chiliocosms within chiliocosms, became a single knife-blade gliding through empty space. What did it matter that his material was slaughtered oxen rather than sounds or colors or words? Nothing remained but the pure joy of the work.

And let's not forget the admirable Wen-hui. Instead of being caught up in princely pursuits like governing, hunting, or dallying with his concubines, there he was in the kitchen, taking exquisite notice of the lowly, which turned out to contain the supreme. When the student is ready, the teacher appears.

15

The ancient Masters
slept without dreaming
and woke up without concerns.
Their food was spare and simple.
Their breath went deep.
They didn't hold on to life,
and they faced death free of concepts,
emerging without desire,
going back without resistance.
They never forgot their beginning;
they didn't trouble their minds
searching for what their end was.
They received life as a gift
and handed it back gratefully.
Minds supple, faces serene,
in a crisis cool as autumn,
in relationships warm as spring,
they were balanced, throughout the four seasons,
and in harmony with the Tao.
There was no limit to their freedom.

COMMENTARY

The ancient Masters had pared themselves down to the essential. They woke up, they ate, they worked, they made love, they raised their families, all the while unseduced by any thoughts that arose. This gave their lives a sense of spaciousness. They always had enough time to do what wanted to be done. They moved through each day as alert and unhurried as animals in the wild.

How could they forget their beginning? That's where they were constantly centered, in the moment before a thought. They had returned to the primordial: mind hovering over its own abyss, objectless, serene. No wonder their nights were dreamless and their skies full of stars. Gratitude makes no distinctions. It precedes its occasion. It is the magic well that never runs dry, the still waters where you kneel and see your own face, more beautiful than you could have imagined.

16

You have heard of flying with wings,
but can you fly without wings?
You have heard of the knowledge that knows,
but can you practice
the knowledge that doesn't know?

Consider a window: it is just
a hole in the wall, but because of it
the whole room is filled with light.
Thus, when the mind is open
and free of its own thoughts,
life unfolds effortlessly,
and the whole world is filled with light.

COMMENTARY

Wisdom is not a something, to grasp or to have. When you discover the extent of your own ignorance, it's like a revelation. "You mean that nothing I believe is true?" Suddenly a window appears in the hermetic chamber. A little openness becomes available. A little humility.

Eventually you realize that there's nowhere the light doesn't penetrate, nowhere the non-wings can't fly.

17

Birth and death, profit and loss,
success and failure, health and sickness—
these qualities are the world
in its constant transformations.
Day in and day out
they vanish into each other
before our very eyes,
and we don't know where they come from.

The Master maintains his balance
whichever opposite he enters.
He lets things go through their changes
and stays focused on what is real.
He is like the ocean:
though there are waves on its surface,
in its depths there is perfect calm.

COMMENTARY

Where can they come from, these bookended qualities, but the projecting mind? The Master is born, he dies; he makes money, he loses money; people love him, they don't; he has the flu, he's better. Amid the transformations of the apparent world, his mind simply observes, curious what will come next, knowing that when we try to grasp anything, it vanishes before our very eyes (as do our very eyes).

All this ungraspability is cause for rejoicing. It's the greatest show on earth: mind realizing its own nature. There's nothing there, and the nothing is beautiful. So of course the Master moves through his life with no problems, saying his yeses and noes with equal amusement, simultaneously waving hello, goodbye.

18

Step beyond yourself.
Step beyond the whole world.
Step beyond all existence.
When you penetrate that far,
you will shine with the original brightness.
You will realize that you are alone
in the vast universe
and that all things are nothing but you.
You will slough off past and present
and will enter the place
where there is neither being nor non-being.

The Master remains peaceful
in the midst of continual change.
There is nothing that can disturb her,
nothing that she finds unacceptable.
She welcomes all beings,
watches as they come and go,
and stays rooted in what is real.

COMMENTARY

This chapter is an accurate description of what happens when body and mind drop away. There is no way to describe the beauty of someone who has penetrated that far.

19

Hui-tzu said to Chuang-tzu, "Do you see that big tree by the roadside? Its trunk is so gnarled and knotted that no one could cut a straight board from it; its branches are so twisted that no one can even measure them. There it stands, and no carpenter bothers to look at it. Your teaching is like that: big and useless. That's why everyone ignores it."

Chuang-tzu said, "Have you ever seen a wildcat stalking its prey? It crouches and waits, it leaps high and low, this way and that, until finally it gets caught in a trap and dies. Or what about a yak? It's as huge as a thundercloud, but it can't catch mice. As for the tree, why don't you plant it in the village of Nothingness, so you can stroll underneath it or take a nap in its shade? No ax will ever shorten its life. If it's useless, nothing can harm it."

COMMENTARY

Chuang-tzu and Hui-tzu, Gilgamesh and Enkidu, Don Quixote and Sancho Panza, Laurel and Hardy—the classic combinations: flint and steel. The line between friend, sidekick, and stooge is fuzzy at best, and it's not glamorous to be the beta male; but without beta, there's no alpha, no act. Keep the ball in play, that's all we ask.

Here Hui-tzu attacks what he sees as a teaching. A teaching? Don't make me laugh! He's like a mosquito biting an iron bull. His criticism is entirely correct, but it's beside the point. Chuang-tzu, however, has already completed his own demolition job. No defense is necessary, because there's nothing left to attack. Like an aikido master, he just steps aside and lets Hui-tzu's own momentum do the trick. He's here, he's there, he's everywhere, conjuring up wildcats, yaks, villages, Nothingness—and suddenly he's back in the spotlight, pulling a red silk handkerchief out of the nose of that elegantly dressed woman in the front row.

We love to see the sage get the best of it, coming to his conclusion like a tonic chord. How can it matter if he's useful or not? He is planted in his own integrity, and there he stands, gnarled and knotted, perfectly at ease with himself, his roots deep in earth, his branches held up to let the light in.

20

The ancient Masters
didn't worry about the future
and didn't regret the past.
When they made a mistake,
they corrected it and moved on;
when they achieved something,
they didn't stop to take credit.
They scaled the heights, never dizzy;
plumbed the depths, unafraid.
Wherever they went in the world,
they were at home.
They realized that the less they knew,
the more they understood.
Thus they embodied the Tao.

COMMENTARY

How cleanly the Master lives, how close to the bone! It's total transparency: what you see is what you get. Since she understands that alternative pasts are only thoughts, she knows that ultimately there are no mistakes in the universe. What happened is what should have happened; there's no other possibility. This insight allows her to confront her own mistakes as soon as they're pointed out. Because they're not personal, she can take full responsibility, correct them, and move on. There's no mental residue: no muss, no fuss.

Nor does she stop to take credit for her achievements. Taking credit would never even occur to her. As if the achievement weren't its own reward. As if, in the freedom of not-knowing, anything were required but the next step.

21

The Master treads lightly on the earth.
Life is not serious for him,
and death is not serious.
Even if the whole world
collapsed, it would not disturb him.
He realizes what is essential.
He has returned to the source.

COMMENTARY

The more we move beyond our ideas about life and death, the more open we are to life. This radical ignorance is not a path to wisdom: it is wisdom itself.

There's a current that is deeper than we are. It will carry us off whether we want it to or not. When we resist it, we suffer. Only when we let it take us can we begin to sense its intelligence.

The Master knows how to die, because he knows how to deal with the everyday losses that form the texture of our life. He deals with them by understanding that loss is just a concept. He looks into the abyss as into the eyes of the beloved.

He knows nothing about death; he knows everything he needs to know about dying.

22

We take on a human body
and delight in what we take on,
and every change
in this constantly changing form
is an opportunity for rejoicing.
The infinite possibilities of the human!

Thus the Master wanders at ease
in a world where nothing is unwelcome.
She delights in sickness and in health,
she delights in an early death,
she delights in old age,
she delights in the beginning,
she delights in the middle and the end.
No experience can happen
that she would exclude or reject.
In this she is like the Tao.
That is why she can serve
as a perfect example for others.

COMMENTARY

Who is the you that takes on a human body? Is it the same you that's left after the body dies? Is *anything* left? Does it matter?

The Master's delight in the never-ending changes of body and world is a remarkable thing. Who would have thought that the mind could be so supple? All things flow; the sun is new every day; it is in change that we find rest. That's why the Master wanders at ease in a world where no experience is excluded or rejected. She knows that the way in and the way out are one and the same. Sickness or health (once the mind has been weaned from comparisons), poverty or riches, a ripe old age, an early death, the beginning, the middle, the end—are equal. She's in love with what is, whatever form it may take.

23

Master Ssu, Master Yu, Master Li, and Master Lai were talking. "Whoever can see non-being as his head, life as his back, and death as his butt, whoever knows that existence and non-existence are one body—that's someone we can be friends with." The four men looked at one another and smiled.

Then Master Yu got sick. Master Ssu went to visit him. "How are you?" he said.

Master Yu said, "Amazing! Look at how the Creator has bent me out of shape. My back is so curved that my intestines are on top of me. My chin digs into my belly button, my shoulders arch over my head, and my neck bones point to the sky." Yet he seemed peaceful and unconcerned. Hobbling over to the well, he looked in and said, "My, my! How totally He has bent me out of shape!"

"Are you discouraged?" asked Master Ssu.

"Not at all," Master Yu said. "Why *should* I be? If things go on like this, maybe He'll change my left arm into a rooster, and I'll announce the dawn. Maybe He'll change my right arm into a crossbow, and I'll shoot a duck for dinner. Or maybe He'll change my buttocks into wheels, and with my spirit for a horse I'll climb up into myself and go for a ride. I won't ever need a wagon again!

"I received life when the time came, and I'll give it back when the time comes. Anyone who understands the proper order of things—that everything happens at exactly the right time—will be untouched by sorrow or joy. In ancient times this was called 'original freedom.' When you argue with reality, you lose. It has always been this way. That's why I have no complaint whatsoever."

COMMENTARY

These four old Chinese sages, who have met in the intimacy
of realization, are like the men whom Yeats saw carved in lapis
lazuli, climbing toward a little half-way house sweetened by
plum- or cherry-branch. Where are Chuang-tzu's men—in a
garden? in a tea shop? The setting doesn't matter. Wherever
it is, whether flowers surround them or falling leaves, I delight
to imagine them seated there, knowing themselves to the core,
saying only what is essential, and smiling in appreciation of the
emptiness at the heart of things.

End of Act One. Act Two is the answer to Job. Perhaps
twenty years have gone by, or twenty days. Master Yu is afflicted
with a neuromuscular syndrome that has bent him over like a
paper clip. "Afflicted"? No: presented; graced. He relates his
symptoms with the aplomb of a pathologist teaching a case
study, a connoisseur describing a masterpiece. No wonder he's
so kind to himself. He had no preconceptions. He doesn't take
the disease personally.

People think that detachment must be a cold, humorless
business. But Master Yu couldn't be more witty or engaging.
Will his left arm turn into a rooster, his right arm a crossbow, his buttocks the wheels of a chariot? Anything can happen, after all, in this world of perpetual transformation, and he
trusts that it will all be turned to good use. His amused segue
into the surreal is a portrait of the mind at ease with itself.

To conclude the dialogue, we're given a statement of what
the Masters are masters of. It's as if the smiles of the four old
men have been transubstantiated into words. Original freedom: the epitome of imperturbability, the gaiety of the mind
that cannot be upset by anything that happens, because at last
it has met itself with understanding.

47

24

To find the Tao,
there is nowhere you need to search.
If it is not inside you,
it is not the Tao.

The Book of Songs says,
When you make the handle of an ax
by cutting wood with an ax,
the model is near at hand.

Thus, in dealing with people,
you already have the perfect
model of behavior inside you.
Just act with integrity,
according to your true nature.
Don't do to others
what you wouldn't want done to you.

COMMENTARY

We talk of inside and outside, but it's as impossible to locate the Tao in the mind as in the world. Anything here or there isn't it. Can your eyes see themselves? When the answer searches for the answer, what can it ever find?

That's why even the most golden rules of behavior don't work, if they're only rules. What is genuine has no models or rules. It's spontaneous, self-generating, free. Nothing can stand against it. It doesn't depend on motivation and isn't concerned with effect. It just wants to be itself, to express itself, to give itself utterly away. Its nature is kindness, but there's nothing moral about it.

In dealing with people, you're always dealing with yourself. The apparent other is you in disguise, the mirrored impulse, the reflection of your own mind, brilliant or confused. Unkindness to the other is literally unkindness to you. When you realize this, you naturally stop hurting yourself. And in the end, you come full circle, where 0° equals 360° and selfishness is an act of pure love.

25

When speaking to people,
you must use words to explain
that reality is beyond words.
You must point to non-being
through being, and describe the whole
through names for the separate parts.
Show them that naming
separates, and that each thing
isn't really itself.
But don't use a finger directly
to show that it's not a finger;
use a non-finger, and they'll see
that a finger isn't a finger.
Don't use a horse directly
to show that it's not a horse;
use a non-horse, and they'll see
that a horse isn't a horse.

Heaven and earth are one finger;
the ten thousand things are one horse.

COMMENTARY

When speaking to a Master, you don't need to use words. You can sit around at a tea shop, for example, and not say anything to each other for hours. A smile is enough. A sip of tea is enough.

When speaking to other people, you can still say everything with a smile or a sip of tea. But if you want to be understood, a skillful relationship with words is important, since reality is beyond words. Though ultimately all you can do is point. Not this, not that.

An ancient Chinese logician explained that, because the word *horse* is color-blind, a white horse is not a "horse." For that matter, a horse is not a "horse." It may be a four-legged animal that neighs, but it is not separate from the rest of non-horsical reality. If anything, it is "reality horsing," or "reality being horsed." I realize that this is getting out of hand. Words are like that. Just when you try to get really serious, words refuse to behave. They just keep horsing around.

So do your best. Keep smiling. Keep sipping. Know from the start that no one will understand. If you come upon a non-finger (as if that were possible), point it in the right direction. If you come upon a non-horse, lead it to water but don't expect it to drink.

26

The Master achieves success,
yet he never does a thing.
His example penetrates the whole world,
yet no one depends upon him.
People don't see him as a leader
since he lets them find their own way.
He stands upon what is fathomless
and walks where no path exists.

COMMENTARY

One of the wonders of what people refer to as spiritual practice (it can also be called "sanity") is that life gets progressively easier. The bumps and jerks, the fumbles and false starts of the apprentice years smooth out, until clarity becomes second nature. Effort is a thing of the past. You're no longer caught in the delusion of making things happen.

Success is whatever is happening right now, and it has no opposite. Someone once asked a Zen Master, "What is the essence of wisdom?" The Zen Master said, "When spring comes, the grass grows by itself."

The great Masters left no precepts, no doctrines, no rules, no traditions, and their words self-destruct upon impact. They had no disciples, because there was nothing to bequeath. They were transparent to their own benevolence, and too kind to offer help. Like the Cheshire Cat, they had vanished down to their smile.

27

Penumbra said to Shadow, "When the Tao moves, you move; when it stops, you stop. Don't you find it depressing to have no power of your own?"

Shadow said, "On the contrary. With no decisions to make, my mind is always at ease. All I have to do is follow. You can't imagine how much freedom there is in just going along for the ride."

Penumbra said, "But how can you know that its decisions are right? Where do you find your trust?"

Shadow said, "Whether I trust it or not—whether or not its decisions are right—when it moves, I move. So I might as well trust it."

COMMENTARY

Darkness is as good a metaphor for spiritual maturity as light is. People talk about "enlightenment," and that describes one facet of the intricate jewel. But you could just as accurately call it "endarkment." We plunge into utter blackness. It becomes very comfortable there.

This little dialogue presents us with Penumbra, the student, and Shadow, the Master, accomplished in the art of stepping out of his own way. Penumbra has some illusory light around his edges: he still thinks he can control what happens. He equates the loss of control with the loss of power. He's projecting on to Shadow what utter powerlessness must feel like. That would depress anyone.

Shadow, for his part, is entirely at the disposal of the intelligence that runs the universe. This makes him a very satisfied fellow. For him, trust is a nonissue. It's peripheral, involuntary, a side effect and fringe benefit of insight. He's the man in the moon, the mirror image, just waiting for reality's eyes to blink or its left hand to touch the tip of its nose. Shadow will blink or touch his nose instantaneously. Fascinating. What will it come up with next?

28

Don't chase after people's approval.
Don't depend on your plans.
Don't make decisions;
let decisions make themselves.
Free yourself of concepts;
don't believe what you think.
Embody the inexhaustible.
Wander beyond all paths.
Receive what you have been given
and know that it is always enough.

The Master's mind is like a mirror:
it responds but doesn't store,
contains nothing, excludes nothing,
and reflects things exactly as they are.
Thus she has what she wants
and wants only what she has.

COMMENTARY

This is a chapter of good advice. You could do a lot worse than follow it. But all advice is dispensable. Here's what I mean.

It's morning again. You open your eyes. There's a you, there's a world. There's even a woman lying in bed beside you, the radiant one, whom you fell in love with the very first moment. The gratitude you feel is one drop in the vast ocean of gratitude that surrounds you. It's unnecessary to feel more than that single drop.

There's a musician at the foot of the bed. His hands look like oak leaves. He is leaning back with his arms raised in a gesture of what might seem (if you didn't know any better) like despair. A skull sits on your nightstand, giving you its long-in-the-tooth, memento-mori grin. Flowers drift through the air in Brownian motion. Inevitably, there's a guitar in your hands. You don't know how to play, but you're a fast learner. It must be time for "La tristesse du roi" or "Amor, la vida es sueño." Your fingers touch the strings. Already you're moved to tears.

Now the sun taps at your window, your bladder needs emptying, the children have dissolved into peals of laughter, and as your feet touch the floor, yet again the spirit of life and death has not a word to say. Do you see things exactly as they are? How would you know? Yet things are so good that they couldn't get much better. All that you ever wanted is here, right in front of you; all that you ever wanted is instantly, irrecoverably, gone.

29

Without the concept of an other,
there is no separate I.
Without the sense of an I,
nothing can be seen as other.
There is some power that determines things,
but I don't know what it is.
It has no form or substance,
acts without doing,
keeps the whole universe in order,
and seems to get along
perfectly well without me.

COMMENTARY

In the mind's spectrum of awareness, solipsism and paranoia are located at about the same point. There's not much difference between an inflated I and an inflated other. Wisdom means no separation. It's easy to keep things at a distance; it's hard to be naturally beyond them. The more intimate you are with yourself, the less anyone can be an other.

The power that determines things isn't me, but it isn't anything else. Realizing this is freedom. It has nothing to do with the credos of religion, those hundred-piece oom-pa-pa bands meant to drown out the sound of doubt. What keeps the whole universe in order speaks with the still small voice of silence. Only the don't-know mind can hear it.

30

The Master accepts his situation
and doesn't want anything else.
If he finds himself rich and honored,
he acts as a rich man should act;
if he is poor and neglected,
he acts as a poor man should act;
in difficulty, he acts as someone
in difficulty should act.
Life can present him
with no situation in which
he isn't master of himself.
When he has a high position,
he doesn't bully his subordinates;
when he has a low position,
he doesn't fawn on his superiors.
He takes responsibility for himself
and seeks nothing from other people,
so he is never disappointed.

Thus the Master
lives in perfect serenity,
arms open to whatever life brings him,
whereas the unaware person
walks on the edge of danger,
continually trying to keep
one step ahead of his fate.

COMMENTARY

The Master lives a life of appropriate action. Because he doesn't believe his own thoughts, there is no barrier between his mind and reality. If he knows to do something, he does it; if he knows not to, he doesn't. Ethics, for him, is so intimate that it has ceased to be a consideration. His peace is as far from the certainty of the arrogant man as from the inner struggle of the good man who doesn't have a clue.

Living in serenity means being open to whatever life brings. When the Master looks forward, there are infinite possibilities; when he looks back, there is only one. What happened is always the best thing that could have happened, because it's the thing that did happen. This is not some Panglossian airy-fairy theory, wishful thinking raised to the nth degree. It's Spinoza's intellectual love of God: rock-solid, incontrovertible, lived.

31

Chuang-tzu and Hui-tzu were playing checkers. "You say that you're an ordinary person," Hui-tzu said. "If you're so ordinary, how can you be so happy?"

Chuang-tzu said, "I'm just like anyone else, except that I don't have feelings like anger, fear, or sadness. Since I don't suffer, 'good' and 'bad' can't affect me."

Hui-tzu said, "Can someone really not suffer?"

Chuang-tzu said, "Of course. When you understand the mind, you're no longer attached to likes and dislikes, so they can't do you any harm. You just follow reality and don't try to control. It's as simple as that."

Hui-tzu said, "But if you don't suffer at all, how can you be human?"

Chuang-tzu said, "Is happiness inhuman? Where does suffering come from? Can it exist outside the mind?"

Hui-tzu said, "But it's unnatural to be happy all the time. Anger and sadness are a part of life. We let go of them as best we can."

Chuang-tzu said, "You have an awfully strange view of the natural. The natural is the spontaneous, the free. When we're clear, anger and sadness can't arise. If you spent less time thinking and more time investigating your mind, you'd stop talking nonsense. How can you let go of what's not there to begin with?"

COMMENTARY

The ancient Chinese form of checkers was a wickedly complicated game. When the two friends played, Chuang-tzu always won, because he had more than logic at his disposal. He could not only see straight ahead; he could see around corners. This gave him a distinct advantage.

Their dialogues were a form of checkers as well. Here the subject is suffering. Hui-tzu believes that anger, fear, and sadness are a necessary part of life, that they spring up out of nowhere, inevitable, uncaused. But every painful feeling is caused by a prior thought. We can't understand the why of the thought's arising, but we can learn the how of undoing it and, with it, our suffering. Then we don't need to bother about the why.

The constant happiness that Chuang-tzu talks about may seem to be an ideal, but in fact he is the realist here. The only thing that can interrupt happiness is an untrue thought. It's like a cloud hiding the sun. When we investigate it, it dissolves. Wisdom is the art of cloudlessness.

32

Reality gives us a body,
thrusts us into the thick
of life and its changing passions,
eases us with old age,
and with death returns us to peace.
And if our life is a good thing,
our death is a good thing too.

COMMENTARY

Having a body isn't a problem, unless you think that you *are* your body. What's the dividing line between inside and outside? The skin? Hmm.

When *good* has no opposite, the mind can't contract into its judgments, and each moment stands by itself, lucid and undeniable. How could death be anything but good, except as the result of a thought? And who would be there to think it?

33

Though the Tao is the realest of the real,
it has no form or substance.
It can be pointed to but not seen,
embodied but not achieved.
It is its own source, its own root.
It is above all things, yet it isn't lofty;
beneath all things, yet it isn't low.
It existed before existence,
began before time began,
and gave birth to birth and death.

Thus the Master isn't fooled
by appearances. He honors
the genuine, wherever it appears.

COMMENTARY

We can call it "God" or "Buddha-nature," we can call it "the mystery at the heart of all things" or "the love that moves the sun and the other stars" or "the vital, immanent, subtle, radiant X." We can get more and more refined, meticulous, or ecstatic, and still it will slip through our language like water through a net. The short version is "the Tao": each thing in the universe seen in itself, each thing *as* the universe, unique, beyond conception.

The less we cling to one side of reality—betting on *either* or *or*, arguing for *for* or *against*—the more we can be aware of the exquisite counterpoint of things. Everything matters: how we vote, how we tie our shoelaces, how we respond to the faintest whisper of a thought. And nothing matters, because (look!) it's already gone. When we understand this, we're home free.

34

The Master lives in the center;
the immature live on the edge
of things, unsatisfied, always
reaching for what is not.

The Master lives in harmony;
the immature pick and choose,
accept some things and reject some,
and make themselves miserable
trying to control the world.

When things seem to be in discord,
return to the center.

The Master lives in the center of the universe, which turned out to be the center of himself. He discovered that there's nothing to it. No self, no other. Amazing! Wherever you go, there you aren't.

The immature live in the center too. It's just that they're not aware of it yet. They put their thoughts between themselves and the center, and presto, they're outside, teetering on the edge of things, looking for love in all the wrong places, trading life and liberty for the pursuit of a happiness that scampers off as soon as it's pursued. A pity.

Actually, it's not a pity, it's a path. Discord becomes opportunity. The center is always less than a thought away.

35

Duke Huan was reading a book at the upper end of the hall. Pien the wheelwright was making a wheel at the lower end. Putting down his mallet and chisel, he walked over and said, "May I be so bold as to ask what Your Grace is reading?"

"The words of the sages," said the duke.

"Are these sages still alive?"

"No, they're long dead."

"Then what you're reading is just the dregs they left behind."

"How dare you make such a comment on what I am reading!" the duke shouted. "Explain yourself, or you die!"

"Certainly, Your Grace," said the wheelwright. "Here's how I see it. When I work on a wheel, if I hit the chisel too softly, it slides and won't grip. But if I hit it too hard, it gets stuck in the wood. When the stroke is neither too soft nor too hard, I know it, my hands can feel it. There's no way I can describe this place of perfect balance. No one taught it to me, and I can't teach it to my son. I have been practicing my craft for seventy years now, and I will never be able to pass it on. When the old sages died, they took their understanding with them. That's why I said that what you're reading is just the dregs they left behind."

COMMENTARY

I don't know who *your* wheelwright is, but these ancient Chinese noblemen had some remarkable folks working for them. Take the ferocious Duke Huan. He was known far and wide for his combustible temper. Drawing a sword was as natural for him as drawing a breath. So you might think that his servants tiptoed around him with their hearts in their throats.

Not in the least. Pien didn't stand on ceremony or wait to be spoken to. He could, after all, have kept on minding his own business, but something in the duke's demeanor called him to intervene. Like a fool, he rushed in where Confucian angels feared to tread. Sometimes you just can't leave well enough alone.

The duke was trying to find the place of perfect balance by reading other people's descriptions. It can't be done. Pien's statement felt like a slap in the face because the duke was still taking things personally. When honor—other people's opinions—is your bread and butter, an insult is a matter of life and death. Fortunately for us, Pien considered life and death to be insignificant matters.

Having uncoiled the tightrope of the duke's anger, Pien proceeded to walk it like an acrobat. This boldness was simply trust in his own experience. He was a man in his eighties, and he knew that what is most valuable can't be taught, it can only be learned.

Marvelously, the story is left open-ended. Pien may well have survived. Maybe the duke nodded in acknowledgment. Maybe he even cried out "Bravo! From the words of this wheelwright, I have learned how to live my life." But if he shouted "Off with his head!" and the sword leapt from its scabbard, Pien would have offered himself without batting an eyelash. Win some, lose some. He was a man fully dedicated to his craft and to the freedom of his perhaps unappreciative sovereign.

36

Whatever happens or doesn't happen,
can you center yourself in the Tao?
Can you stop looking to others
and focus on your innermost self?
Can you return to the beginning of the world
and be like a newborn baby?
It can scream its head off all day,
yet it never becomes hoarse.
It can clench its fist for hours,
yet its fingers never get cramped.
It can stare all day without blinking,
yet its eyes never grow tired.
Free from concerns and worries,
unaware of itself,
it moves without thinking,
doesn't know why things happen,
doesn't need to know.

To act without needing a reason,
to sit still without knowing how,
to ride the current of what is—
this is the primal virtue.

COMMENTARY

People think that entering the kingdom of heaven has something to do with good and evil. But as Jesus implied, every mother's child wakes up in the kingdom of heaven. Heaven is intimacy: the world before separation. It looks exactly like earth, but without the thoughts that branch out in a thousand directions too heavy for us to bear.

Our first parents were not the good children in a morality tale. They were enchanted with each other and with themselves, Adam staring into the mirror of phenomena, Eve singing as she plaited a wreath. The tree they ate from was not called the Tree of Evil: it was the Tree of the Knowledge of Good and Evil. They became mere grown-ups the moment they bit into that bitter fruit. They opened their eyes and thought that they knew something. They heard the voice of guilt and punishment walking in the garden in the cool of the day. They imagined that they were naked, when all the while they were clad in all earthly abundance, and crowned with the moon and stars.

37

Though the Master does nothing,
her not-doing is the opposite of inaction.
Because she acts without effort,
each task does itself, in its own time.
Her body may move or not move,
but her mind is always at ease.

Still water is like a mirror:
when you look into it,
you can see the very hairs on your eyebrows.
It lies so horizontal
that carpenters use it as a measure.
If water is so clear, so level,
how much more so the Master's mind!
All things are reflected in it
as they are, without distortion.
It is like the Tao,
open, serene, unmoving,
the mirror of heaven and earth.

COMMENTARY

The Master does what everyone else does—gets up, brushes her teeth—but she isn't stuck in the thought that's she's doing it. This makes her life very simple. Tic-tac-toe.

Her mind is always at ease, because she doesn't believe that reality should be different than it is, right now. She's the field of awareness, the fulcrum of the possible. She's the placeholder, the space-giver, the word on the tip of your tongue. When you read between the lines, it's her that you're reading. She's the mirror and the mirrored, the pond and the servant kneeling, the truth-teller, the self-knower, the self-delighter, the lover of what is, the one with the wide-open heart, the one you can always depend on. She's no one. She's you without a future. She's the you you always wanted to be.

38

Chuang-tzu and Hui-tzu were walking across the bridge over the river Hao. Chuang-tzu said, "Look at the minnows, swimming and leaping to their hearts' content. That's what makes fish happy."

Hui-tzu said, "You're not a fish, so how do you know what makes fish happy?"

Chuang-tzu said, "You're not me, so how do you know that I don't know what makes fish happy?"

Hui-tzu said, "True, I'm not you, so I certainly have no idea what you know. On the other hand, you're certainly not a fish, and that just proves that you can't know what makes fish happy."

Chuang-tzu said, "Let's go back to your original question. You said, 'How do you know what makes fish happy?' So when you asked the question, you knew that I knew it. I know it by standing here over the river Hao."

COMMENTARY

Chuang-tzu and Hui-tzu, old pals and sparring partners, are at it again. Crossing the river, Hui-tzu stirs things up from a less-than-radical not-knowing. Logically, he has the better case. But the conversation isn't about knowing. (Chuang-tzu would be the first to concede that he can't know anything.) The real topic is freedom. If what you hear is two men arguing about who's right, you've missed the point.

An apocryphal sage named Einstein—who could easily have been photographed in an ebullient mood, with his tongue out—said, "There is only one important question: Is the universe friendly?" Here's another way of putting it: When the mind is happy, the universe is happy. Does the universe seem unfriendly or neutral? It's only because you're seeing it that way.

As Chuang-tzu watches the minnows swimming and leaping, his heart leaps too. Naturally he projects his own joy onto them. He's happy for them, *as* them. And who's to say that this is not an accurate view of reality? For all we know, the whole universe is alive and pulsing with joy, joy pulsing from every minnow, every molecule, from every creature on earth, from fire, hail, snow, and frost, mountains and barren hills, fruit trees and cedar forests, wild animals and tame, reptiles, insects, and birds: joy to the world, all the boys and girls, joy to the fishes in the deep blue sea, joy to you and me.

39

The Master lets go of desire
and people are fulfilled;
he has no goal in mind
and people are transformed;
he remains silent
and people are educated.
Act without doing,
speak without intention,
and even the beggars in the street
will benefit from your example.

The Master doesn't interfere.
He perfects the whole world in his heart.
He leaves the gold hidden in the mountains
and the pearl at the bottom of the sea.
He has no interest in wealth or fame,
sees no advantage in long life,
isn't elated by success,
isn't discouraged by failure
or confused by the world's rights and wrongs.
He knows that all beings
are strung on a single thread
and that life and death are one body.

COMMENTARY

The Master's job couldn't be cushier. All he does is be, and he doesn't even do that. There's nothing required of him. He doesn't help, doesn't lead, doesn't set an example. He just observes the marvelous transformations of mind. When we live or work with him, we are inspired by his very presence, by the spaciousness of it. Finally, someone who is at home in the world, who's utterly responsible and carefree. We didn't know it was possible to be happy all the time. We didn't know you could have a heart without any checkpoints.

The Master doesn't interfere in other people's lives. Why would he? He knows that he doesn't know what's best for the world, or even for himself. He leaves the gold hidden in the mountains, because he doesn't need it on his wrist or around his wife's neck or in the bank. Yes, he could buy pickaxes and hire ten villages of dwarfs, but he realizes that when you extract gold there's always an irritated dragon to deal with. Besides, entrepreneurship is less exciting than the adventure of discovering what is enough. How fine life becomes when what you want is exactly what you have!

40

Are you worried about the world?
Do you think that it needs your guidance?
Don't the heavens turn by themselves?
Don't sun and moon find their places?
What masterminds all this?
What creates all the connections?
What, without any effort,
makes everything happen in its time?
Is there some hidden mechanism
that makes life be as it is?
Do things just happen to turn out
exactly the way they do?
Do clouds make the rain, or is it
rain that makes up the clouds?
What force puffs them and punctures them?
The winds rise in the north,
they blow now west, now east,
and wander across the heavens.
What, without any effort,
stirs up this unfathomable joy?

COMMENTARY

Some people have an Atlas complex: they carry the world on their shoulders. They believe that if they put the world down, it couldn't carry on by itself. Worry and fear, they think, are the motivators for right action. If they saw the world as perfect, they think, they would be complacent and passive: they would just stay at home and cultivate their own gardens.

But what if cultivating your own garden were the best way to help the world? What if your little backyard could, with the proper care, grow enough vegetables and fruits to feed a million people? What if your gardening inspired a thousand of your neighbors to do the same? —"But a backyard can't feed a million people." —Ah, my dear fellow, it's a metaphor. I'm not talking about physical food, or even, necessarily, physical people.

Worrying about the world is a dead end. When nuclear proliferation is solved, global warming pops up. When global warming is solved, overpopulation starts looming. Then there's always the burning out of the sun, and the infinite expansion or contraction of the universe, which leaves us at zero any way you slice it.

When the mind discovers what it is, we wake up from these mortal dramas as if from a dream. All possible disasters have already happened, and if a future appears, we thread it through the eye of the needle. And whether we act or don't act, voilà: miraculously, without exception, things turn out exactly the way they do.

41

In the beginning, there was nothing.
From nothing arose the One.
All things return to it.
Because it is without form,
there is no way to name it.
It doesn't exist and doesn't
not-exist. When we call it "the Tao,"
we define nothing as a something.

The Tao is beyond words.
The more you talk about it,
the farther away from it you get.
Only when you are truly
unattached to words or to silence
can you express the truth.

COMMENTARY

Ah, the Tao, the Tao. When we talk about it, the vast isn't vast enough, and the subtle seems ludicrously crude. The only way to approach it is through paradox: to step out of the way until language bites its own tail. And a little chutzpah doesn't hurt.

Chutzpah is usually defined as "effrontery," but it's more than that. It's effrontery with a feather in its cap, it's the sound of three hands clapping, it's a garlic bagel crashing a party of champagne flutes. It's not a good thing or a bad thing, but we tend to smile or gasp when we encounter it. Though there's no Chinese ideogram for *chutzpah*, this chapter is a perfect case study.

So: if the more we talk about the Tao, the farther away from it we get, why would we talk about it at all? But okay, let's talk. We begin with the beginning, which equals zero, a nice round number that is the absence of numbers. From this absence, the One arises. Are you reeling yet? But there's more. If zero transmutes into one, zero equals one. (So much for the foundations of mathematics.) Then, from the One, after a fraction of a nano-instant, with a bang, the infinitely many arise. Ultimately infinity returns to the One, which equals zero. But the One doesn't not-exist. It doesn't exist either; you can't limit it to either category of mind. So when we say, "All things are one," we're lying through our teeth. Since reality is beyond conception, how can we dare to talk about it?

But we do. And there's something endearing about the daring of that. If nothing else, it makes us think. Even better, it makes us not-think, which could be the point of it all.

42

As Chuang-tzu was fishing in the river P'u, two high officials arrived from the king of Ch'u and said, "Sir, the king requests that you come to the capital and serve as his prime minister."

Without turning his head, Chuang-tzu answered, "I have heard that in Ch'u there is a sacred tortoise that died three thousand years ago. The king keeps its shell in the temple, wrapped in silk and encased in a golden box. Now if you were this tortoise, would you prefer to be venerated in such a way, or would you rather be alive again, crawling around in the mud?"

"The latter, certainly," said the officials.

Chuang-tzu said, "Give my compliments to His Majesty, and tell him that I am happy right here, crawling around in the mud."

COMMENTARY

This story features Chuang-tzu as Huckleberry Finn. All he needs for perfect contentment is a fishing pole and some bait. It's easy to decline power when you don't care what people think of you and you've unraveled the urge to control. There's nothing more delicious than having no future.

The king of Ch'u was a little slow on the uptake, because he didn't understand how useful it is to be useless. The job of prime minister was the pinnacle of success for a commoner, the worldly man's daydream. It was also a royal pain in the neck: long hours, stupefying details, dangerous boss, ungrateful public.

Having delivered the king's request, the officials waited politely. They were wise men and knew that fishing is not about catching fish. Chuang-tzu didn't bow, he didn't rise to face them; his behavior could have been considered the height of rudeness. But integrity is always beautiful to the discerning eye. His focus was on the fishing pole. He never even stopped to wonder about the consequences of a refusal.

In the end, the officials returned to Ch'u not empty-handed. What they respectfully carried back was Chuang-tzu's response, which was, in their eyes, an honor to the king. It was also an honor to the sacred tortoise, brought back to muddy life now after three thousand years.

43

Give up wanting to be important;
let your footsteps leave no trace.
Travel alone as the Tao
to the land of the great silence.

If a man is crossing a river
and an empty boat
collides with his own boat,
he won't get offended or angry,
however hot-tempered he may be.
But if the boat is manned,
he may flare up, shouting and cursing,
just because there's a rower.

Realize that all boats are empty
as you cross the river of the world,
and nothing can possibly offend you.

When you understand how utterly alone you are, it's a cause for celebration. Break out the caviar and champagne! *Le roi est mort, vive le roi!*

If everyone is your projection in the first place—if you see not them but who you think they are—how can you be offended? Scene: a river. You're drifting along in your little boat, happy as a minnow, and suddenly some jerk bangs into you, full force. But when you look, it's an empty boat. Since there's no offender, naturally there's no offense. —"You mean that the woman who broke my heart, or my backstabbing colleague, or the politicians who got us into this mess, they're all empty boats?" —"Yes, indeed." This has nothing to do with taking the right action against greed or stupidity. But if you're offended, it means that you're not paying attention.

44

Chaff from the winnowing fan
cancels the eye's natural vision;
the whine of a mosquito
can keep you awake all night;
trying to be benevolent
makes the mind a tangle of confusion.
If you want the world to stay simple,
you must move with the freedom of the wind.
Why keep making the effort
to figure out right and wrong?
Why all this huffing and puffing
as though you were beating a drum,
searching for a lost child?
The snow goose doesn't need
a daily bath to stay white,
nor does the crow stay black
by dipping itself in an inkwell.
When the springs dry up
and the fish are left on the shore,
they spew one another with moisture.
But how much better if they could
forget one another and swim off
into the lake's vast freedom!

COMMENTARY

The effort to be moral or benevolent is a disruption of our natural virtue. What child would rather pray than play? "Throw away morality," Lao-tzu says, "and you'll be doing the world a big favor." Trying to figure out the right action does no one any good. It's better to keep moving, till the right action arises by itself.

When it's genuine, benevolence is the most beautiful quality in the world. But when it has a motive, it feels like fish spittle, not like clear water. We recognize the genuine. It's what we all want. It's what we all are, when we see past our own thoughts. Let the others comfort one another with slime: that's the best they can do under the circumstances. But the instant any fish finds its way back to the lake, it will swim off without a qualm. "Thanks for the benevolence, muchachos, but I'm out of here."

45

Everything, seen in itself,
is both good and bad, right
and wrong, useful and useless,
appropriate and inappropriate,
possible and beyond possibility.
A battering ram
can break down a city wall,
but it can't patch a hole in the ceiling.
Fine horses can travel
a hundred miles in a day,
but they can't catch mice as a weasel can.
The owl can spot a flea
in the dark, but in broad daylight,
however hard it may stare,
it can't even see a mountain.

If you want to have right without wrong
or order without disorder,
you don't understand the Tao.
You can't have one quality
and not have its opposite as well.
You can't reach for the positive
and not create the negative
by the very act of your reaching.

The Master stands beyond opposites.
She doesn't move toward or away.
She sees things exactly as they are.

COMMENTARY

In itself, everything is free of qualities, but when it appears to you or me, it absorbs qualities from the mind, as a color absorbs light. The tree that moves some to tears of joy is, for others, only a green thing that stands in the way. As we see it, so it is.

Once you realize that for every thought you believe, the opposite is equally true, there's no way you can get stuck. "Give me a place to stand on," Archimedes said, "and I will move the earth." How can you make the world right if you're standing in the midst of right-and-wrong? Having vowed to overcome entropy, you create order at point A, and immediately point B collapses into chaos. You reach out toward the shadowless, and the closer your hand gets, the closer your shadow gets, too.

The Master understands that in the moral universe, as in the physical, the observed depends on the observer. This leaves her with no place to stand. From this no-place, she can move the whole universe.

46

Ch'ing the master woodworker carved a bell stand so intricately graceful that all who saw it were astonished. They thought that a god must have made it.

The Marquis of Lu asked, "How did your art achieve something of such unearthly beauty?"

"My Lord," Ch'ing said, "I'm just a simple woodworker—I don't know anything about art. But here's what I can tell you. Whenever I begin to carve a bell stand, I concentrate my mind. After three days of meditating, I no longer have any thoughts of praise or blame. After five days, I no longer have any thoughts of success or failure. After seven days, I'm not identified with a body. All my power is focused on my task; there are no distractions. At that point, I enter the mountain forest. I examine the trees until exactly the right one appears. If I can see a bell stand inside it, the real work is done, and all I have to do is get started. Thus I harmonize inner and outer. That's why people think that my work must be superhuman."

COMMENTARY

When people saw Ch'ing's bell stand, they were astonished to get a glimpse of who we are. Awe is the natural reaction to genius: a recognition, an unforeseen depth. Explanations are secondary. People thought that a god must have made the bell stand only because they imagined a limit to the human mind. Like Duke Huan's wheelwright and Prince Wen-hui's cook, Ch'ing had learned to follow the Tao, which goes beyond all art. Without the distraction of past or future, his mind was free, moment by moment, to move toward its own delight. Concentration, he found, was not a matter of applying effort; it was a way of eliminating the unnecessary. After a while, concepts such as good and evil, success and failure, flitted off into the unreal like ghosts that have lost their mission. What remained was the silence, a deep slow-flowing river in which he stood up to his hips, attentive to every ripple and splash, knowing that there was a hidden life beneath the surface and that if only he was patient enough, it would yield itself to him in its time. Nothing happened for days, and again nothing, and more nothing, and he was unaware of how tenuous the separation between him and the world had become.

By the time he entered the forest, he was a tree among trees. Coming upon the right one was like seeing himself in a mirror. Suddenly it was there, *he* was there, and the bell stand fully articulated within him. From that point on, he knew he would never die.

47

You can't talk about the ocean
with a frog who lives in a well:
he is bounded by the space he inhabits.

You can't talk about ice
with an insect who was born in June:
he is bounded by a single season.

You can't talk about the Tao
with a person who thinks he knows something:
he is bounded by his own beliefs.

The Tao is vast and fathomless.
You can understand only by stepping
beyond the limits of yourself.

You *can* talk about the ocean with a frog who lives in a well, but the conversation will be rather one-sided. Eventually you realize that the only reason you've been talking is that you love the sound of your own voice.

"Let me tell you about the ocean. It's vast. It's deep."

"Huh?"

"You can sail across it for days, for weeks, and never come to the end."

"Yeah. Right."

"It contains trillions of quadrillions of living creatures, from the microscopic to the gargantuan."

"I have a few lily pads here. Flies and mosquitoes."

"The ocean is so deep that fish living far down generate their own light."

"What do you mean by 'fish'?"

48

Let go of all your assumptions
and the world will make perfect sense.
In movement, be fluid as water;
at rest, be bright as a mirror;
in response, be simple as an echo.
Keep your mind serene,
like the still surface of a lake.
Clear-eyed and imperturbable,
walk through life
as though you didn't exist.
When nothing is left to argue with
and there is nothing to oppose,
you will find yourself at peace
and in harmony with all things.

COMMENTARY

Our assumptions about the world become our world. Confusion projects confusion, and we wonder why life doesn't make sense. "Why do the wicked prosper?" That's easy: because they do. If this answer seems flippant, you might take a closer look at *wicked* and *prosper*. There are assumptions in each word that can put you in a padded cell or inspire you to exterminate your neighbors.

But if assumptions are questioned deeply enough, they let go of themselves. The world becomes intelligible, kind, and problem-free, because the mind has become clear. Your you is no longer a something; it's fluid, permeable, bright, it winks in and out of existence like a quark. When you find nothing to oppose, there's nothing that can oppose you.

49

Chi Hsing-tzu was training a gamecock for the king. After ten days, the king asked if the bird was ready for combat. "No, Your Majesty," said Chi. "He's arrogant, always ready to pick a fight. He's still relying on his own strength."

Another ten days passed, and the king asked again. Chi said, "No, Sire, not yet. He still becomes excited when a rival bird appears."

Ten more days. The king asked again. "Not yet," Chi said. "He still gets an angry glint in his eye."

Another ten days, another question. Chi said, "Now, Sire, he's almost ready. When a rival crows, he doesn't react. He stands motionless like a block of wood. His focus is inside. Other birds will take one look at him and run."

Yes, yes, I know that blood sports are immoral. But just for a moment, let's posit a world in which they're not only moral but heroic. If, in that world, you were a trainer of gamecocks, wouldn't you want to do your job without a scruple? What for someone else would be animal abuse would for you be the training of the supreme athlete, the ultimate competitor. Rather than lounging around the barnyard and ending up roasted on a platter for a merchant's Sunday dinner, your birds would be rigorously cared for, brought to the peak of fitness, given a life of privilege and abundance punctuated by a few violent, satisfying murders. For the weaker ones, the end would be quick: instead of a butcher's knife, an adrenaline rush and the flash of a rival's spur.

Chi Hsing-tzu was an expert. He was in the business of turning ordinary roosters into feathered samurai. This took an austere hand, a keen eye, and a spiritual discernment that even a Master might admire. There was no barrier between trainer and trained. Since he didn't rely on his own strength, he could easily spot arrogance in others. Since his own heart was calm, he could sense when the slightest agitation arose in his birds. What other trainers might miss—the too-confident strut, the glint of impatience or anger—his awareness was quick to pounce on.

The point was to step into the ring indifferent to life and death, with no desire for success or fear of failure. Entirely concentrated, the graduate of Chi's training walked forward sensing neither self nor other. The lesser champions fought and won. The great champions didn't have to fight; they were masters of the art of peace, and their opponents could find nowhere to penetrate. In the face of such magnificence, discretion was the better part of valor.

50

The mature person is like a good archer:
When he misses the bull's-eye,
he turns around and seeks
the reason for his failure in himself.

COMMENTARY

When you can live this most radical simile, "missing the bull's-eye" may look like a flash of irritation with your wife, or outrage at the morning's headlines. "Turning around" means taking total responsibility. There's no blame or denial in it.

51

Unchain yourself from achievement
and enjoy an ordinary life.
Flow like the Tao, unhindered,
unnoticed, unnamed,
with no goals, no expectations.
Be like a child, like a fool.
Know that there is nothing to know.
This is the direct way to freedom.

COMMENTARY

Only because our perspective is so limited do we think we can achieve something that lasts. To a more expansive mind, a billion years are but as yesterday. Eternity laughs at the productions of time. In the bardo realm, seeing the lone and level sands under which his mighty works lay buried, Ozymandias decided that the next time around, he would be a shoemaker in the Bronx.

Achievements and attainments are just stories of a future or a past. Right now, in this moment, there is—there can be—nothing but the ordinary: a man sitting at the kitchen table with a cup of lukewarm coffee in front of him. Not much to achieve *there*. The day unfolds its little surprises, you flow from concentration to relaxedness to concentration, from morning to evening, and the only possible break in the current of delight is an untrue thought. Everyday mind is the Tao.

52

The duck's legs are short; you can't lengthen them
without making her suffer.
The crane's legs are long; you can't shorten them
without causing him pain.
What is long needs no cutting off;
what is short needs no stretching.
When you realize this,
you can let the world go its own way.
Do you think that you know what's best?
Do you think that the world
should conform to your way of thinking?
All these benevolent people—
how much worrying they do!
Since ancient times,
what a lot of fuss and upheaval
the benefactors of humanity have caused!

COMMENTARY

We don't usually imagine benevolent people as wreaking havoc right and left. And yet, if you contemplate this chapter, you may come to see a world in which ducks are stretched out on the rack with nothing to confess but their shortness, and amputee cranes line the highways on crutches, each with a tin cup, begging for alms. This may be a world closer than you think. It may be your life.

Even with the kindest of intentions, you can't try to change people without inflicting violence on them and on yourself. Hitler and Stalin, in their own opinions, were acting for the benefit of humanity. They thought that they knew best. Violence was a necessary prelude to Utopia. In order to make an omelet, you had to crack a few eggs. This is how the I-know mind functions. It's lethal.

Whenever I believe that you are too much or not enough, I am caught in a delusion, and I suffer. Those ducks—they're perfect just the way they are, waddling around on their adorable little legs. And cranes stride through the marsh on legs not a millimeter too long. There may be a lot that needs fixing, but there's nothing out there to fix.

53

As he was eating by the side of the road, Lieh-tzu saw an old skull. He pulled it out of the weeds, contemplated it, and said, "Only you and I know that there is no such thing as death and no such thing as life."

COMMENTARY

The philosopher Lieh-tzu has stopped for lunch on his journey from here to there. He sits down by the side of the road, opens his knapsack, takes out a few rice balls and a piece of dried fish. It's a leisurely meal. He has nowhere in particular to go. Suddenly he notices an old skull. He pulls it out of the weeds for a tête-à-tête. He has no ideas about whoever used to inhabit it, no pity, no urge to do an "Alas, poor Yorick." The skull is his colleague. It may look a bit hollow, but it knows exactly what he knows.

"You too," Lieh-tzu says, "have no mind to contend with. You don't tell yourself lies about pain multiplied beyond one body. You realize that death is a noun without a plural. Only one person ever dies."

"If that," says the skull, a master of understatement.

54

The Book of Songs says,
The hawk soars to the heavens,
the fish plunges to the depths.
This means that there is no place
where the Tao doesn't penetrate.

For the mature person,
the Tao begins in the relation
between man and woman, and ends
in the infinite vastness of the universe.

The Tao doesn't need to penetrate anywhere. It's already there. (*There* is here.) You could say that there's nowhere it isn't, and yet there's nowhere it is. But how abstract these concepts of space and time are! Perhaps some Native American language has a single word for *that through which all perceptible forms manifest,* a word as vivid as the green of grass or the smell of an orange. Awareness is what matters. If the awareness that the universe is intelligent doesn't penetrate into my blood, my bones, I might as well not have it.

The mature person is the student of the mind, the one who understands that reality happens from the inside out. What are we projecting? The relation between man and woman is the clearest mirror. When we get that right, we get everything right.

55

Life is the companion of death;
death is the beginning of life.
Who can understand
how the two are related?
But if life and death are companions,
why should you be concerned?
All things are connected at the root.
We arrive here from the unknown
and go back to where we came from.

What people love about life
is its miraculous beauty;
what they hate about death
is the loss and decay around it.
Yet losing is not losing, and decay
turns into beauty, as beauty
turns back into decay.
We are breathed in, breathed out.
Therefore all you need
is to understand the one breath
that makes up the world.
The Master is always conscious
of the mystery at the heart of all things.

COMMENTARY

After the joyful raucous skepticism of the earlier chapters—a bucketful of ice water poured onto you while you're still snoozing under the comforter—this chapter's mode of unknowing is a grandmotherly kindness. Life becomes very gentle when you understand that you're not living it.

56

The ancient Masters looked ordinary,
but their wisdom was profound.
They didn't deviate from the truth.
The clever couldn't persuade them,
the beautiful couldn't seduce them,
the rich couldn't corrupt them.
They considered life and death
to be insignificant matters.
Unhindered, their minds could soar
to the edges of the unknown,
beyond time and space, and plunge
past the beginning and the end.
They could take the most menial positions
and find contentment in their work.
Their virtue filled earth and heaven.
The more they gave to themselves,
the more they could give to others.
The more they gave to others,
the more they had for themselves.

COMMENTARY

You never knew when you'd bump into one of them. You might be in a public toilet and there he was, scrubbing the floor, humming to himself with a little smile. Or you'd be buying a piece of salmon at the market, and the fat old woman behind the counter would ask an ungraspable question that would resonate inside you for days. Or you'd sit down next to a beggar on the street, one of the lost apparently, his wrinkles caked with grime, and when he looked into your eyes, you'd feel penetrated to the core.

The ancient Masters had no word for compassion. They wouldn't have understood it, because they didn't harbor concepts of "self" and "other." Generosity, for them, was like breathing. When they gave, it was for no reason, to no one. They didn't expect a grateful response, or any response at all. It was always themselves they were giving to.

57

Once, when a seabird landed outside the capital, the Marquis of Lu escorted it to his ancestral temple, had the music of the Ninefold Splendors performed, poured out a cup of old wine, and spread before it a feast of beef and pork. But the bird became dazed, and it pined away, refusing to taste meat or wine. In three days it was dead.

This was treating the bird as the marquis would have liked to be treated, not as the bird would have liked to be treated. Had he done so, he would have let it roost in the deep forests, play among the islands, swim in the rivers and lakes, feed on mudfish and minnows, fly with the rest of the flock, and live any way it chose to.

COMMENTARY

The capital of Lu must have been seriously landlocked if this seabird (an albatross perhaps) seemed so exotic. The bird was a sensible creature, and the last thing it wanted was celebrity. The marquis, a famous epicure and an obtusely empathetic fellow, proceeded to kill it with kindness. He chose the best of everything, but the bird was not impressed by the ancient Chinese equivalents of a 1947 Cheval Blanc, a three-star Michelin meal, and the Goldberg Variations. It died pining for its freedom and a couple of fresh fish.

The marquis was not the only person in history who, by acting out the Golden Rule, became the golden fool. Was he repentant afterward? Did he start buttonholing wedding guests and holding them with his glittering eye? In any case, the extravagance of his selfishness removes him from history and inserts him into parable. Any child can tell you that hay is for horses, milk is for cats, and fish is for albatrosses, and that we should let wild animals live any way they choose to. Love your neighbor as yourself: leave him alone.

58

If you center yourself in non-being,
your mind becomes one.
If your mind has become one,
there is no opening in you
through which harm can enter.

When a drunk falls from a wagon,
he won't be killed, no matter
how fast the wagon is moving.
His body is like other men's,
but the way he falls is different.
Life and death mean nothing to him;
thus fear can't enter his heart.
He meets all circumstances
like an infant, without a thought.
Unconscious that he is falling,
he falls softly, and his bones
bend like the branches of a tree.

If there is such safety in wine,
how much more in wisdom!

COMMENTARY

Drunks can teach us a lot. For example, that the road of excess leads to the forest of confusion. Or that without the thought of a future, we always fall softly. That's a good thing to know. Life is an ongoing course in learning how to fall. The falling is inevitable; the harm is optional.

59

As you simplify your mind,
you will see how simple life is.
As you learn not-knowing,
your heart will find its way home.
Content as a suckling infant,
mindless as a newborn calf,
you will no longer exhaust yourself
looking for impossible answers
and wandering in search of *Why?*
You will come to rest in the Tao,
happy with what life brings you.

COMMENTARY

Given a choice between being Einstein and being a newborn calf, most people would choose the former. But this chapter is not about stupidity versus intelligence. There's a great deal of intelligence in the mindlessness of a newborn calf, which is further along in its self-reliance than a newborn baby, even a baby Einstein. The calf, in fact, knows everything it needs to know. All the important questions are answered for it, forever.

"Simplify, simplify," our friend Thoreau said. He could simply have said, "Simplify," since a word to the wise is sufficient. But for our unwisdom, he raised the decibel level. He may even have had to shout at Einstein, who was a master of simplicity, though not of simplifying his own life. All honor to him, and yet he would have given his eyeteeth to understand the mind of God, which every newborn calf or suckling infant can manage. A Theory of Everything? What is is. How simple can it get?

60

There is nothing more perfect than the Tao,
yet it doesn't seek perfection.
When you understand perfection,
you realize that there is nothing to seek,
nothing to gain or lose,
nothing to defend or reject.
You return to yourself
and find what is inexhaustible.

For most of us, perfection is an idea of what should be. Comparing what is to our idea of what should be, we judge what is as deficient. But once we get a little sanity going and can tell the difference between reality and our thoughts about it, the habit of comparison subsides, and perfection becomes not abstract but lived. In the first flush of understanding, we may feel drunk with the good news, we may have to pinch ourselves, we may start babbling the obvious, in the words of the ancient poet: "This is perfect. That is perfect. Perfect comes from perfect. Take perfect from perfect, the remainder is perfect."

The unattainable—how close it is! No need to understand it or accept it, no need to look anywhere else, or to look for it at all. How can it be lost if it was ours from the very beginning? How can it be found if it was never lost?

61

Chuang-tzu's wife died. When Hui-tzu came to offer his condolences, he found Chuang-tzu sprawled out on the ground, pounding on a tub and singing.

Hui-tzu said, "You loved her all these years, you lived with her, you brought up your children and grew old together. Now that she's gone, don't you owe her a few tears, or at least silence? But pounding on a tub and singing at the top of your lungs—that's a bit much, don't you think?"

"Not at all," Chuang-tzu said. "When she died, I mourned as anyone else would. But then I looked back to the root of her being: not just before she was born, but before she even had a body; not just before she had a body, but before she had a soul. In the midst of the unfathomable ever-changing mystery, suddenly, out of nowhere, she had a soul. Then, suddenly, she had a body. Then, suddenly, she was born.

"Now there has been another transformation, and she's dead. The same process that brought her to birth, in time brought her to death, as naturally as fall turns into winter and spring into summer. Now she is lying at peace in her vast room. I realized that if I went around wailing and pounding my chest, it would show that I didn't understand the first thing about reality. So I stopped."

COMMENTARY

Chuang-tzu's wife died at exactly the right time, as do we all. She moved on without the impediment of concern for her husband, knowing that he wouldn't feel a moment's grief for her. This made her very happy.

Now, in the period of mourning, Chuang-tzu sits sprawled out on the ground, pounding on a washtub and singing. He enjoys singing loudly, with gusto. He isn't a great drummer, but he has a certain odd rhythm of his own. The woman he loves has never left; nothing of her is missing but the body. How can a merely physical absence affect his joie de vivre?

Hui-tzu, as usual, comes onto the scene as the perfect straight man. His is the voice of shocked piety, the propriety that holds the corners of the universe in place with laundry pins. *If you don't suffer,* he thinks, *it means that you don't care.*

In his reply, Chuang-tzu is the soul of patience. It's amazing what lies come out of his mouth. He speaks as though he had waited for his wife to die in order to understand about death. That would have been to close the barn door after the horse was stolen.

Actually, his whole account of gradual discernment is a fairy tale to cushion the shock to his friend's sensibilities. This is called "skillful means"; if he bent over backward any farther, his ears would be touching his ankles. In reality, there was no mourning, no looking back, no realization, no stopping. Chuang-tzu's wife died. He loved her. He was a happy man.

62

In an age when the Tao is followed,
no one rewards the talented
or pays special attention
to the lovely, the virtuous, or the wise.
Those who govern
are simply the highest branches
on the tree, and the people wander
in freedom, like deer in the woods.
They are honest but think nothing of it,
they naturally do what is right,
they are kind without any conception
of kindness, and are trustworthy
though they wouldn't know what that means.
They keep no records of their good deeds,
because good deeds are so common.
That is why all their actions
have vanished, without a trace.

Excellence is its own reward. When we picture a golden age in which everyone has woken up from the dream of ego, we realize that a simple thank-you is enough—more than enough. But even though, from the standpoint of the excellent, rewards are unneeded, governing well is like being a good parent: no one in the family is left out. As Alice's Dodo says, *"Everybody has won, and all must have prizes."*

This doesn't mean that we abandon discernment and let in the rule of cant. How can Salieri's art equal Mozart's, or Rosa Bonheur's, Cézanne's? Genius isn't democratic. A monument to great Jewish hockey players? Once, at a dinner party, Dr. Johnson said that he could recite an entire chapter from Horrebow's *Natural History of Iceland*: "Chapter 72, *Concerning Snakes*. There are no snakes to be met with throughout the whole island."

Yeats wrote about a peasant girl so beautiful that farmers jostled at the fair to get a glimpse of her. There *is* something awe-inspiring about beauty, as about virtue or wisdom. Yet when you're married to a beautiful woman, it's nothing special; she's beautiful in the same way that the grass is green. Not that you don't deeply appreciate her beauty, but it's part of your daily landscape. It's both numinous and familiar, both ho-hum and halleluyah.

We read reports of a hero leaping onto the subway tracks to save someone from an oncoming train. A moment before, he couldn't have predicted that. There was no thought involved, it was a not-doing, the Tao just took over. And when he tells a reporter, "I'm no hero; anyone would have done the same," he could be right.

63

The Book of Songs says,
Though the fish sinks to the bottom,
it still can clearly be seen.

Thus the Master
examines her innermost self.
She notices even the smallest
sign of discord, and corrects it
before it can do any harm.

When your mind is transparent to the depths
and your words and actions are one,
the whole world becomes transparent.

The Master does more than just *notice* discord in herself. Since she knows that a feeling of discord can only be caused by a prior thought, she questions the thought. For her, discord is always a momentary imbalance. When it is investigated, it unravels. Thus it can never do any harm. This is not ethics; it's mental hygiene. When the mind is transparent, the heart is transparent. There are no beliefs to keep awareness from shining through.

The primal light shines through even the densest matter. As the world becomes transparent, your goodness, and everyone's, is gradually, heart-stirringly revealed. To the transparent eye, there is no place where goodness is not. When a pickpocket sees a saint, he sees only his pockets; when a saint sees a pickpocket, he sees only his innocence.

64

Integrity is our true nature;
arriving at integrity
is the work of a lifetime.

The person who has integrity
does the right thing without trying to,
understands the truth without thinking,
and naturally embodies the Tao.

Integrity is not only
the fulfillment of our own being;
it is also the quality
through which all beings are fulfilled.
When we fulfill our own being,
we become truly human;
when we fulfill all beings,
we arrive at true understanding.
Humaneness and understanding
are inherent in our nature,
and by means of them
we unite the inner and the outer.
Thus, when we act with integrity,
everything we do is right.

COMMENTARY

Integrity is the bridge to the kingdom, the kiss that wakes the dead princess, the fingers that spin straw into gold. When a person has integrity, she's genuine; you can always trust that her yes is a yes and her no a no. There's no motive behind it, no sweet sticky lure for approval.

We love integrity. It feels like home. It's solid, there's no acting-out in it, no backtracking, no second-guessing. When you act with integrity, everything you do is right, because there's no separation between doer and done. Besides, you realize that you're not doing it in the first place. You have let go into the nameless, and it's not even you who have let go. It's not even you who have been let go of.

NOTES

FOREWORD

page xi **two Chinese anthologies:** This pairing might have seemed illegitimate to scholars of a generation ago. But since excellence is horizontal, not vertical, it feels more appropriate to group the best of these texts according to insight, not according to tradition. Besides, at the time they were compiled there was no rigid dichotomy between Taoist and Confucian. "Any simplistic division of the spectrum of ancient Chinese philosophy into narrowly defined competing 'schools of thought' loses sight of the deep fount of issues, assumptions and common lore shared—and freely exchanged—by pre-Ch'in thinkers of virtually every ideological stripe" (Andrew Plaks, *Ta Hsüeh and Chung Yung*, p. 80).

page xi **the Chuang-tzu:** The basis for all extant editions is the recension by Kuo Hsiang (c. 300 CE), who abridged an earlier anthology from fifty-two to thirty-three sections and arranged them in the order we have today.

page xi **parts of which were written by the eponymous sage:** The traditional view is that the first seven sections (known as the "inner chapters") were written by him, and the rest of the book by his students and followers. But in fact it's impossible to know which passages were written by Chuang-tzu himself. I would bet that the brilliant section 2 originated with him and that most of the stories about him didn't. In the end, all we can say is that the inner chapters contain passages of clarity, wit, and great spiritual depth, and others that are silly and dull. In the outer chapters the proportion of dullness increases, but even there, especially in sections 17–19, we find passages that equal the best of the first seven sections.

page xi **Master Chuang:** *Tzu* means "Master." The only details we have about his life come from Ssu-ma Ch'ien's *Historical Records* (c. 104 BCE), which states that he came from Meng (probably in present-day Honan), that his surname was Chuang and his given name Chou, and that he once served as an official in the "lacquer garden" in Meng.

page xi **Chung Yung:** This could also be translated as "The Doctrine of Moderation" or "The Balance Between Polarities." Pound's title is "The Unwobbling Pivot."

page xi **Tzu-ssu:** His personal name was K'ung Chi. Almost nothing is known about him. All we're told is that he was Confucius' grandson and Mencius' teacher and that he lived in the ancient country of Lu (present Shantung province).

page xiii **a Zen poet-descendant:** Zen Master Hsueh-tou (980–1052), compiler of the famous koan collection *The Blue Cliff Record*.

ABOUT THE ADAPTATION

page xv **Octavio Paz:** *Chuang-Tzu,* p. 14.

page xvi **a particular elegance to it:** Even the innumerate, like me, may get a kick out of knowing that 81 is a perfect totient number, a heptagonal number, a centered octagonal number, a tribonacci number, an open meandric number, the ninth member of the

Mian-Chowla sequence, and, in base 10, a Harshad number and one of three numbers that, when its digits are added together, produces a sum that, when multiplied by its reversed self, yields the original number (information according to wikipedia.org).

page xvi **so does 64:** 64 is the smallest number with exactly seven divisors, the lowest positive power of 2 that is adjacent to neither a Mersenne prime nor a Fermat prime, the sum of Euler's totient function for the first fourteen integers, a dodecagonal number and a centered triangular number, and a self number—i.e., an integer that in a given base (in this case, base 10) cannot be generated by any other integer added to the sum of its digits (wikipedia.org).

page xvi **the only two-digit number ever to star:** Other two-digit numbers have, at best, supporting roles: 10 in "All Together Now" and in "Being for the Benefit of Mr. Kite!," 15 in "She Came In Through the Bathroom Window," 17 in "I Saw Her Standing There," and 50 and 31 in "Maxwell's Silver Hammer." (The only other number that stars in a major song happens to be the square root of 64.)

CHAPTER 1 (Chung Yung, 1)

page 2 **The Tao is the way things are:** Minus our thoughts about the way things are.

page 2 **which you can't depart from / even for one instant:** A most profound statement. —"You mean it's impossible to do it wrong?" —That's what he's saying.

page 2 **looks into her own heart:** What you don't see inside, you can't see outside. If there is chaos in your mind, the world seems chaotic; if your mind is clear, the world, with all its apparent horror, can't help but appear as beautiful. When you can rest in the space before thought, you understand the Tao without substance, the reality that is above, beneath, before, after, and always now.

CHAPTER 2 (Chung Yung, 1)

page 4 **Before sorrow, anger:** It's equally true to say that after sorrow, anger, yearning, or fear have arisen, you are in the center; you've just lost the awareness of it.

page 4 **heaven and earth take their proper places:** In the I Ching, heaven over earth (12) is the hexagram for stagnation, whereas earth over heaven (11) is the hexagram for peace.

COMMENTARY

page 5 **There's no one else you can save:**

> Any bodhisattva who undertakes the practice of meditation should cherish one thought only: "When I attain perfect wisdom, I will liberate all sentient beings in every realm of the universe, and allow them to pass into the eternal peace of Nirvana." And yet, when vast, uncountable, unthinkable myriads of beings have been liberated, truly no being has been liberated. Why? Because no bodhisattva who is a true bodhisattva entertains such concepts as "self" or "others." Thus there are no sentient beings to be liberated and no self to attain perfect wisdom.
>
> —*The Diamond Sutra* (4th century CE)

CHAPTER 3 (Chuang-tzu, 2)

page 6 **It is the inexhaustible treasury:**

> When Hui-hai first came to Ma-tzu, the Zen Master asked him, "What have you come here for?"

Hui-hai said, "I have come seeking the Buddha's teaching."

"What a fool you are!" Ma-tzu said. "You have the greatest treasure in the world inside you, and yet you go around asking other people for help. What good is this? I have nothing to give you."

Hui-hai bowed and said, "Please, tell me what this treasure is."

Ma-tzu said, "Where is your question coming from? This is your treasure. It is precisely what is asking the question at this very moment. Everything is stored in this precious treasure-house of yours. It is here at your disposal; you can use it as you wish; nothing is lacking. You are the master of everything. Why then are you running away from yourself and seeking for things outside?"

Upon hearing these words, Hui-hai realized his own mind.

COMMENTARY

page 7 **Every ism is a wasm:** Abbie Hoffman (1936–1989).

page 7 **don't-know mind:** The wonderful phrase of Zen Master Seung Sahn (1927–2004).

CHAPTER 4 (Chuang-tzu, 2)

page 8 **When we exhaust our minds:** It's exhausting to be right all the time.

page 8 **A monkey trainer:** He's not only a master of communication, he's a master of strategy.

page 8 **The monkeys were outraged:** These monkeys are intelligent enough to understand Chinese, but not enough to understand their own minds. There is always something to be outraged about, from the trivial to the cosmic, from the selfish to the compassionate. The rage is always extra.

page 8 ***All right, then:*** A masterstroke.

page 8 ***The monkeys were delighted:*** But a good lawyer might have gotten them five in the morning and two in the afternoon.

page 8 ***Nothing essential had changed:*** It never does.

page 8 ***knew how to adapt to reality:*** The opposite of manipulation. He's so flexible that he can instantly adjust his position.

page 8 ***harmonize with both sides:*** He sees both sides as counterpoint.

page 8 ***walking on two paths at once:*** By putting one foot in front of the other.

CHAPTER 5 (Chuang-tzu, 2)

page 10 ***The ancient Masters saw deeply:*** They saw as deeply as they needed to, because they looked past their own thinking.

page 10 ***This is perfect understanding:***

> If you don't live the Tao,
>   you fall into assertion or denial.
> Asserting that the world is real,
>   you are blind to its deeper reality;
> denying that the world is real,
>   you are blind to the selflessness of all things.
> The more you think about these matters,
>   the farther you are from the truth.

Step aside from all thinking,
and there is nowhere you can't go.
—Seng-ts'an (?–606), "The Mind of
Absolute Trust" (trans. Stephen Mitchell)

page 10 **saw no boundaries between them:** Still, I am impressed.

page 10 **saw boundaries / but didn't judge things as good or bad:** I don't have a problem with that.

page 10 **understanding was damaged:** Not because judgments arose, but because people believed them.

page 10 **preferences became ingrained:** "The Great Way isn't difficult," Seng-ts'an wrote, "for those who are unattached to their preferences." One scoop of vanilla, please.

COMMENTARY

page 11 **The opposite of a profound truth is another profound truth:** Niels Bohr (1885–1962).

page 11 **"All Cretans are liars," said the Cretan:** The Epimenides paradox, named after the Cretan philosopher Epimenides of Knossos (c. 600 BCE).

page 11 **All the world's a stage:** *As You Like It*, II.vii.

page 11 **there's nothing left but gratitude and laughter:** This is a quotation from my wife, Byron Katie. Other quotations and echoes include: "there is no beginning of time, only a beginning of thought" (10), "there are no mistakes in the universe" (20), "She's in love with what is, whatever form it may take" (22), "When you argue with reality, you lose" (23), "When the Tao moves, you move"

(27), "What happened is always the best thing that could have happened, because it's the thing that did happen" (30), "every painful feeling is caused by a prior thought" (31), "He knows that he doesn't know what's best for the world, or even for himself" (39), *"If you don't suffer,* he thinks, *it means that you don't care"* (61).

CHAPTER 6 (Chuang-tzu, 2)

page 12 **Everything can be seen as a this**: And thus separate from everything else.

page 12 **You can't have right without wrong:** The mind that creates right simultaneously creates wrong.

page 12 **nothing is absolute:** Realizing this is the beginning of humility.

CHAPTER 7 (Chuang-tzu, 2)

page 14 **Nothing in the world is bigger:**

> There is no here, no there;
> infinity is right before your eyes.
> The tiny is as large as the vast
> when objective boundaries have vanished;
> the vast is as small as the tiny
> when you don't have external limits.
>
> —Seng-ts'an

page 14 **the tip of an autumn hair:** "The strands of animal fur were believed to grow particularly fine in autumn" (Watson's note).

page 14 **Mount Everest:** Literally, "Mount T'ai," in Shantung province, the first of the five sacred mountains of China; its tallest peak is Jade Emperor Peak (5,069 feet).

page 14 is tiny: "If we consider their forms," wrote Kuo Hsiang (252?–312), the ancient editor of the Chuang-tzu, "Mount T'ai is obviously larger than an autumn hair. But if all things simply are what they are, and fully accept their limitations, then even the largest is not too large, and the smallest is not too small. Being satisfied with how it is, the autumn hair does not see its own smallness as smallness, nor does Mount T'ai see its own largeness as largeness. If being large enough is called large, nothing in the world is larger than the autumn hair. If not being large enough is called small, even Mount T'ai could be small. In truth, there is no absolute largeness, no smallness, no long life, no premature death."

page 14 **Methuselah:** Literally, "P'eng-tsu," the great-grandson of Emperor Chuan Hsu; according to legend, he had ninety wives and was eight hundred years old when he departed for the West.

page 14 **The universe came into being / the moment that I was born:** Finally, an honest man.

> The truth is that everything comes from the I. If there's no thought, there's no world. Without the I to project itself, there is neither origin nor end. And the I just appears: it doesn't come out of anything and it doesn't return to anything. Actually, even "nothing" is born out of the I, because even it is a concept.
>
> —Byron Katie, *A Thousand Names for Joy*

page 14 **what happens / when we move from being to being?** Infinity is what appears when zero looks in the mirror.

page 14 ***It's better just to leave things alone:*** Well, I certainly hope you've learned your lesson.

CHAPTER 8 (Chuang-tzu, 2)

page 16 ***in the middle of a dream:***

> The sage (*jñāni*) dreams, but he knows it to be a dream, in the same way as he knows the waking state to be a dream. Established in the state of supreme reality, he detachedly witnesses the three other states—waking, dreaming, and dreamless sleep— as pictures superimposed onto it. For the sage, all three states are equally unreal. Most people are unable to comprehend this, because for them the standard of reality is the waking state, whereas for the sage the standard is reality itself.
>
> —Ramana Maharshi

COMMENTARY

page 17 ***they know even as they are known:*** 1 Corinthians 13:12.

page 17 ***We are close to waking up when we dream that we are dreaming:*** Novalis (Friedrich von Hardenberg, 1772–1801), *Blütenstaub*, 17.

CHAPTER 9 (Chuang-tzu, 2)

page 18 ***Then he woke up:*** He *apparently* woke up. This begs the question, of course.

page 18 ***there he was again:*** Only if he believed the memory of a past. Actually, there he was for the first time.

page 18 was he Chuang-tzu…: Was he a present believing a past, or a past believing a present? This is getting rather complicated.

page 18 There must be some difference: Oh, really?

page 18 This is called "the transformation of things": Plus ça change, plus c'est la même chose.

COMMENTARY

page 19 Feynman diagram: In 1949 Richard Feynman showed that an antiparticle (such as a positron) going forward in time may be viewed as a particle (such as an electron) going backward in time. This symmetry is built into the visual aids called Feynman diagrams that are used by physicists to calculate the rates of various reactions between elementary particles.

CHAPTER 10 (Chuang-tzu, 2)

page 20 There was a beginning of time: Okay, if you say so.

page 20 There was a time before the beginning / of time: Here we go.

page 20 There was a time / before the time before / the beginning of time: Stop, stop, I'm getting dizzy!

page 20 There is being: What about the ancient Masters, with their perfect understanding that nothing exists? Have we slid down to the next stage so quickly?

page 20 If there is being, there must be / non-being: In for a penny, in for a pound.

page 20 If there is non-being, / there must have been a time when even / non-being didn't exist: That's what you get for fooling around with opposites.

page 20 **Suddenly there was non-being:** Whoa!

page 20 **But can non-being really exist, / and can being not-exist?:** Yes. Next question.

page 20 **I just said something:** Who said you just said something? Must you always live in the past?

CHAPTER 11 (Chuang-tzu, 2)

page 22 **doesn't avoid failure:** What other people might call failure. But because failure is just a judgment superimposed onto reality, he has no reason to avoid any experience. When you don't aim for "success," how can you fail?

page 22 **doesn't act with a motive:** As if there were rules for the genuine.

page 22 **and remains pure / amid the world's dust and grime:** What dust and grime? Since her own mind is pure—that is, free of its own thoughts—she can only project purity onto the world.

page 22 **She lets the confused stay confused:** Everything in its own time.

page 22 **and is always available / to those with a passion for the truth:** They ask, she answers. They answer, she asks.

page 22 **she is content with not-knowing:** More than content: She is delighted.

COMMENTARY

page 23 **When I attained unexcelled perfect enlightenment:** The Diamond Sutra. (The Buddha of this scripture is a character invented by the Mahayana imagination.)

CHAPTER 12 (Chung Yung, 26)

page 24 **transcends all things:** It isn't a thing.

page 24 **at the heart of all things:** It isn't separate.

page 24 **creates without doing:** This is the miracle. The least bit of doing, and it's gone.

page 24 **fulfills without an intention:** An intention would be a limit.

COMMENTARY

page 25 **Who doesn't think that light is beautiful:** "Yes, light. But what does it shine on? It is beautiful even when it shines on nothing. And when it shines on evil? Even then it is beautiful; even when it shines on what is hideous." —Joseph Joubert (1754-1824)

page 25 **Whatever the self describes, describes the self:** Jakob Boehme (1575-1624).

CHAPTER 13 (Chuang-tzu, 2)

page 26 **Things are the way they are / because we think they're that way:** Nothing can exist, as it is perceived, without the perceiving mind. There's no objective "out-there"; each of us creates the world in his own image.

page 26 **all things are good and acceptable:**

> If the mind is happy, not only the body but the whole world will be happy. So you must find out how to become happy yourself. Wanting to reform the world without discovering your true self is like trying to cover the whole world with leather to

avoid the pain of walking on stones and thorns. It
is much simpler to wear shoes.

—Ramana Maharshi

page 26 *the person of true vision:* The person who sees, beyond
thought, that everything is perfect just the way it is. "Perfection,"
Spinoza said, "is another name for reality" (*Ethics*, IV, preface). He
also said, "Anyone who is free can form no concept of good and
evil" (*Ethics*, IV, Prop. LXVIII).

COMMENTARY

page 27 *"There is nothing either good or bad but thinking makes it so":*
Hamlet II.ii. If Hamlet had understood his own words, he would
have lived happily ever after. (This would have been a major
problem for Shakespeare.)

page 27 *a hundred ways:* Lao-tzu, for example:

> When people see some things as good,
>   other things become bad.

—Tao Te Ching, 2

page 27 *on the evening of the sixth day:* "And God saw everything that
he had made, and, behold, it was very good" (Genesis 1:31). This
state of mind is known as Sabbath.

CHAPTER 14 (Chuang-tzu, 3)

page 28 *Prince Wen-hui:* Possibly King Hui of Wei (370–319 BCE).
The historical character was a grandson of Marquis Wen of Wei,
the founder of the state, and helped the economic growth of his
country by moving the capital from Anyi to Daliang.

page 28 **the dance of the Mulberry Grove:** A rain dance said to date from the time of T'ang, who founded the Shang dynasty in 1766 BCE.

page 28 **the chords of the Lynx Head music:** A composition said to date from the time of Yao (2358–2258 BCE), another legendary king.

page 28 **"Well done!" said the prince:** Is this the first time he has seen his cook at work? Or is he paying attention for the first time?

page 28 **Putting down his knife, Ting said:** Ting not only knows how to do not-doing, he knows how to speak about doing not-doing.

page 28 **I follow the Tao:** There's no distance between the follower and the followed.

page 28 **[all I could see was] the ox:** A large hunk of dead matter.

page 28 **I had learned to look beyond the ox:** It was no longer an ox; it was the whole universe.

page 28 **Nowadays I see with my whole being:** His eyes have become telescopes, microscopes.

page 28 **I slow down:** It slows down; *it* focuses my attention.

page 28 **and let the joy of the work fill me:** How generous of him!

page 28 **Then I wipe the blade clean and put it away:** The joy is just the next-to-last step.

page 28 **"Bravo!" cried the prince:** He can't help crying out in admiration, dazzled as if before a great work of art, like Rilke contemplating the archaic torso of Apollo: "here there is no place / that does not see you. You must change your life."

COMMENTARY

page 29 **the Buddha proscribed trafficking in meat:** Anguttara Nikaya 5:177.

page 29 **How can we know the dancer from the dance?:** Yeats, "Among School Children."

page 29 **chiliocosms:** In Buddhist cosmology, the world system that we can perceive is a *small world*; a thousand small worlds form a *small chiliocosm*, a thousand *small chiliocosms* form a *medium chiliocosm*, and a thousand *medium chiliocosms* form a *great chiliocosm*, which thus consists of a billion *small worlds* like ours. There is an infinite number of *great chiliocosms* in the universe.

page 29 **When the student is ready, the teacher appears:** This has been called "old adage," "old Indian saying," "Buddhist proverb," "Chinese proverb," "old Zen saying," etc., but no one has identified the source.

CHAPTER 15 (Chuang-tzu, 6)

page 30 **The ancient Masters / slept without dreaming:** They didn't bother to dream. This made things simpler for their students. No banquets. No butterflies.

page 30 **woke up without concerns:** Just like the lilies of the field.

page 30 **didn't hold on to life:** They could take it or leave it. They treasured life to the utmost, but they weren't attached to it.

page 30 **emerging without desire, / going back without resistance:** Nothing ventured. Nothing gained.

CHAPTER 16 (Chuang-tzu, 4)

page 32 but can you fly without wings?: Not until you've overcome the gravity of habitual thinking.

page 32 the knowledge that doesn't know:

> All bodhisattvas should develop a pure, lucid mind that doesn't depend upon sight, sound, touch, flavor, smell, or any thought that arises in it. A bodhisattva should develop a mind that alights nowhere.
>
> —*The Diamond Sutra*

page 32 free of its own thoughts: This doesn't mean that stressful thoughts don't appear. It's just that you no longer believe them. Thus they have no power.

CHAPTER 17 (Chuang-tzu, 5)

page 34 they vanish into each other: They define each other, support each other, depend on each other, follow each other, become each other.

page 34 He lets things go through their changes: They go through their changes whether or not he lets them. When Margaret Fuller announced to Thomas Carlyle, "I have accepted the universe," Carlyle said, "Egad, Madam, you'd better!"

COMMENTARY

page 35 curious what will come next:

> Apart from the pulling and hauling stands what I am,
> Stands amused, complacent, compassionating, idle,
>   unitary,

Looks down, is erect, bends an arm on an impalpable
    certain rest,
Looks with its sidecurved head curious what will come
    next,
Both in and out of the game, and watching and
    wondering at it.
                    —Walt Whitman, "Song of Myself"

CHAPTER 18 (Chuang-tzu, 6)

page 36 the original brightness:

> In its true state, mind is naked, immaculate,
> transparent, empty, timeless, uncreated, unimpeded;
> not realizable as a separate thing, but as the unity
> of all things, yet not composed of them; undif-
> ferentiated, self-radiant, indivisible, and without
> qualities. Your own mind is not separate from
> other minds; it shines forth, unobscured, for all
> living beings.... Without beginning or ending,
> your original wisdom has been shining forever, like
> the sun. To know whether or not this is true, look
> inside your own mind.
>   —*The Tibetan Book of the Great Liberation* (8th century CE)

page 36 you are alone / in the vast universe: That is, you are completely
at home in the vast universe.

page 36 the place / where there is neither being nor non-being:

> A monk asked Zen Master Tung-shan, "When
> heat and cold come, how can we escape from
> them?"
> Tung-shan said, "Why don't you go to the place
> where there is neither heat nor cold?"

The monk said, "What place is that?"

Tung-shan said, "When it is hot, you die of heat. When it is cold, you die of cold."

page 36 **There is nothing that can disturb her:** Epictetus (c. 55–c. 135) wrote, "We are disturbed not by what happens to us, but by our *thoughts* about what happens." Nothing on the apparent outside can disturb us. When thoughts are comfortable, mind has to be comfortable, because mind is thoughts; it doesn't exist without them. (When it doesn't exist, it's even more comfortable.)

CHAPTER 19 (Chuang-tzu, 1)

page 38 **Hui-tzu** (Master Hui, a.k.a. Hui Shih; c. 380–305 BCE). The foremost logician of the time. He also appears in chapters 31, 38, and 61 here.

page 38 **no carpenter bothers to look at it:** It would be a total failure as a tree if trees grew to suit carpenters.

page 38 **That's why everyone ignores it:** As well they should. It's a way of life. If they think it's a teaching, they're in big trouble.

page 38 **Have you ever seen a wildcat stalking its prey?** Huh? How did we get on to wildcats?

page 38 **gets caught in a trap and dies:** Wait a minute! Are you saying that the wildcat gets caught because it has a purpose? Does it *necessarily* get caught? Does *every* wildcat end up in a trap, bleeding to death? Are there no wildcats who die old and full of days, surrounded by their cubs and grandcubs?

page 38 **Or what about a yak:** Ah, now we're in Tibet. I'm cutting you some slack here, Chuang, trying to zig where you zig. But you're zagging.

page 38 **It's as huge as a thundercloud, but it can't catch mice:** No, that would be a wildcat. At least the yak doesn't get caught in a trap and die.

page 38 **why don't you plant it in the village of Nothingness:** Yes, I can do that. And before the tree has grown tall, I can stretch out in the shade of a yak.

CHAPTER 20 (Chuang-tzu, 6)

page 40 **didn't worry about the future / and didn't regret the past:** They knew the difference between what is and what isn't.

page 40 **They scaled the heights, never dizzy:** They never looked down.

page 40 **plumbed the depths, unafraid:** They realized that the deeper they went, the less fear there could be.

CHAPTER 21 (Chuang-tzu, 5)

page 42 **The Master treads lightly on the earth:** Because he takes himself lightly. He no longer believes any thoughts about what should be, so he is perfectly comfortable with what is. And because he realizes that what is is already gone, there's nothing to hold him in place. Realization: the antigravity machine.

page 42 **Life is not serious for him:**

> The face of the wise man is not somber or austere, contracted by anxiety and sorrow, but precisely the opposite: radiant and serene, and filled with a vast delight, which makes him the most playful of men.... If someone has experienced the wisdom that can only be heard from oneself, learned from oneself, and created from oneself, he

does not merely participate in laughter: he becomes
laughter itself.

—Philo of Alexandria (c. 20 BCE–c. 50 CE)

page 42 *it would not disturb him:*

> He who correctly realizes that all things follow
> from the necessity of the divine nature, and come to
> pass in accordance with the eternal laws and rules
> of nature, will not find anything worthy of hatred,
> derision, or contempt, nor will he bestow pity on
> anything, but to the utmost extent of human virtue
> he will try to do well and to rejoice.
>
> —Baruch de Spinoza, *Ethics*, IV, Prop. L, Note

CHAPTER 22 (Chuang-tzu, 6)

page 44 *an opportunity for rejoicing:*

> When a man feels that he exists in the world as
> in a great, worthy, and beautiful whole, when this
> harmonious ease affords him a pure delight, then
> the universe, if it could experience itself, would
> shout for joy at having attained its goal, and admire
> the pinnacle of its own essence.... For what end is
> served by all the expenditure of suns and planets
> and moons, of stars and milky ways, of comets and
> nebula, of worlds evolving and passing away, if at
> last a happy man does not involuntarily rejoice in
> his own existence?
>
> —Johann Wolfgang von Goethe

page 44 *No experience can happen / that she would exclude or reject:*
"To men, some things are good and some are bad. But to God,

all things are good and beautiful and just."—Heraclitus (c. 535–c. 475 BCE) (Diels-Kranz 102).

COMMENTARY

page 45 **All things flow; the sun is new every day; it is in change that we [lit., things] find rest:** Heraclitus (Plato, *Cratylus* 402a; Diels-Kranz, 6, 84A).

page 45 **The way in and the way out are one and the same:** "The way up and the way down are one and the same."—Heraclitus (Diels-Kranz 60).

CHAPTER 23 (Chuang-tzu, 6)

page 46 **Master Ssu, Master Yu, Master Li, and Master Lai were talking:** It was a short conversation. They got right to the point.

page 46 **looked at one another and smiled:** What a delight when someone else knows that ultimately nothing matters. *I* don't matter? Brilliant! Now we can really meet.

page 46 **the Creator:** That's one way of putting it. Let's project a personal god, an intention, to see if even a trace of resentment can be found.

page 46 **Why should I be?:** The only way he could be discouraged is if he believed a thought like "This shouldn't be happening."

page 46 **everything happens at exactly the right time:** To suppose anything else is insane.

COMMENTARY

page 47 **the men whom Yeats saw:** W. B. Yeats, "Lapis Lazuli."

CHAPTER **24** (Chung Yung, 13)

page 48 **there is nowhere you need to search:** "This thing we tell of can never be found by seeking, yet only seekers find it." —Abu Yazid al-Bistami (?–c. 874).

page 48 **If it is not inside you, / it is not the Tao:** How simple can this get?

page 48 **The Book of Songs:** Each one could be subtitled "Song of Myself."

page 48 **Don't do to others / what you wouldn't want done to you:** The angle of incidence equals the angle of reflection.

COMMENTARY

page 49 **Can your eyes see themselves?:** An old Hindu and Buddhist saying.

CHAPTER **25** (Chuang-tzu, 2)

page 50 **When speaking to people:** Zen Master Lin-chi (?–866) said, "I have no teaching to give people. All I do is untie knots."

page 50 **point to non-being / through being:** Being arises from non-being as matter arises from the vast universe of dark matter. Or is that just one more story?

page 50 **describe the whole:** "The whole" is a name for a separate part.

page 50 **they'll see / that a finger isn't a finger:** Ceci n'est pas une pipe.

page 50 **Heaven and earth are one finger:** Which points back to you.

COMMENTARY

page 51 **Not this, not that:** "The description of Brahman [the Godhead, or Absolute Reality] is: 'Not this, not that.' There is no more appropriate description." —Brihadaranyaka Upanishad (8th–7th century BCE)

page 51 **An ancient Chinese logician:** Kung-sun Lung (c. 320–250 BCE), whose most famous work is *Treatise on the White Horse.* In it, he observes that "we don't use the term 'horse' to identify horses on the basis of color—that is why it is possible to include black or yellow horses in the term 'horse'; but we use the expression 'white horse' to identify horses on the basis of color—that is why it is not possible to include black or yellow horses in the term 'white horse.' Since 'white horse' distinguishes what 'horse' does not, a 'white horse' is not a 'horse.'"

CHAPTER 26 (Chuang-tzu, 7)

page 52 **he never does a thing:** He doesn't have to.

page 52 **His example penetrates the whole world:** Whether or not the world knows it.

page 52 **People don't see him as a leader:**

> When his work is done,
> the people say, "Amazing:
> we did it, all by ourselves!"
>
> —Tao Te Ching, 17

p. 52 **He stands upon what is fathomless:** As we all do.

COMMENTARY

page 53 **a Zen Master:** Yün-men (?–949).

CHAPTER 27 (Chuang-tzu, 2)

page 54 *All I have to do is follow:* That's all anyone ever does, all anyone *can* do. It's just that Shadow is aware of it.

page 54 *I might as well trust it:* Trust is the default condition. You can't distrust it unless you're believing an untrue thought about it.

CHAPTER 28 (Chuang-tzu, 7)

page 56 *The Master's mind is like a mirror:*

> QUESTION: What does mind resemble?
>
> ANSWER: Mind has no color, is neither long nor short, doesn't appear or disappear; it is free from both purity and impurity; it was never born and can never die; it is utterly serene. This is the form of our original mind, which is also our original body.
>
> QUESTION: How does this body or mind perceive? Can it perceive with eyes, ears, nose, touch, and consciousness?
>
> ANSWER: No, it doesn't use means of perception like that.
>
> QUESTION: Then what sort of perception is involved, since it isn't like any of the ones already mentioned?
>
> ANSWER: It is perception by means of your own nature. What does this mean? Because your own nature is pure and utterly serene, its immaterial and motionless essence is capable of this perception.
>
> QUESTION: But since that pure essence can't be found, where does this perception come from?

ANSWER: We may compare it to a mirror which, though it doesn't contain any forms, can nevertheless reflect all forms. Why? Because it is free from mental activity. If your mind were clear, it wouldn't give rise to delusions, and its attachments to subject and object would vanish. Then purity would arise by itself, and you would be capable of such perception. As the Dharmapada Sutra says, "To establish ourselves amid perfect emptiness in a single flash is the essence of wisdom."

—Zen Master Hui-hai (8th century CE),
On Sudden Awakening, trans. John Blofeld

CHAPTER 29 (Chuang-tzu, 2)

page 58 nothing can be seen as other:

> In the world of things as they are,
>   there is no self, no non-self.
> If you want to describe its essence,
>   the best you can say is "Not-two."
> In this "Not-two" nothing is separate,
>   and nothing in the world is excluded.

—Seng-ts'an

page 58 I don't know what it is: What a relief!

page 58 keeps the whole universe in order:

The scientist's religious feeling takes the form of a rapturous amazement at the harmony of natural law, which reveals an intelligence of such superiority that, in comparison with it, the highest intelligence of human beings is an utterly insignificant reflection.

—Albert Einstein

page 58 *and seems to get along / perfectly well without me:* So far, so good.

COMMENTARY

page 59 **It's easy to keep things at a distance; it's hard to be naturally beyond them:** Zen Master Bunan (1603–1675).

CHAPTER 30 (Chung Yung, 14)

page 60 *accepts his situation:* This isn't something you can decide to do. You can try to think positively till you're blue in the face, but underneath the thoughts you want to believe, what thoughts are you actually believing?

page 60 **If he finds himself rich and honored:** His favorite situation.

page 60 **if he is poor and neglected:** His favorite situation.

page 60 **in difficulty:** Now this is getting really interesting.

page 60 **He takes responsibility for himself:** Ah, that's the point!

page 60 **and seeks nothing from other people:**

> A monk asked Zen Master Tao-wu, "How can I keep a clear mind?"
> Tao-wu said, "If a thousand people call you and you don't turn your head, you can say you have achieved something."

page 60 **walks on the edge of danger:** On the edge of *apparent* danger, never realizing that he is perfectly safe.

page 60 **one step ahead of his fate:** As if he can outrun his own shadow.

COMMENTARY

page 61 **the best thing that could have happened:**

> When you have what you want—when you *are* what you want—there's no impulse to seek anything outside yourself. Seeking is the movement away from the awareness that your life is already complete, just as it is. Even at moments of apparent pain, there's never anything wrong or lacking. Reality is always kind; what happens is the best thing that could happen. It can't be anything else, and you'll realize that very clearly if you inquire.
>
> —Byron Katie, *A Thousand Names for Joy*

CHAPTER 31 (Chuang-tzu 5)

page 62 **Hui-tzu:** Him again! I hope he has let go of that thing about uselessness.

page 62 **were playing checkers:** Each sentence is a move. Though Chuang-tzu invariably wins, Hui-tzu isn't a sore loser; he keeps coming back for more: a testimonial to the strength of their friendship.

page 62 **Can it exist outside the mind?:**

> I sometimes say that you move totally away from reality when you believe that there is a legitimate reason to suffer. When you believe that any

suffering is legitimate, you become the champion of suffering, the perpetuator of it in yourself. It's insane to believe that suffering is caused by anything outside the mind. A clear mind doesn't suffer. That's not possible.

—Byron Katie, *A Thousand Names for Joy*

page 62 **it's unnatural to be happy all the time:** "What is now proved was once only imagined." —William Blake, *The Marriage of Heaven and Hell*

page 62 **Anger and sadness are a part of life:** An unexamined assumption.

CHAPTER 32 (Chuang-tzu, 6)

page 64 **thrusts us into the thick / of life:** Where else can we begin to undo ourselves?

page 64 **eases us with old age:** We are eased when the life force weakens: a kind experience for those who value clarity.

page 64 **and with death returns us to peace:** To the state before being and non-being.

CHAPTER 33 (Chuang-tzu, 6)

page 66 **it has no form or substance:** Like a law of physics.

page 66 **embodied but not achieved:** Everything you do reflects it, yet it's nothing you can do.

page 66 **It existed before existence:** Well, okay. Still, he can't get very far walking around with his foot in his mouth.

COMMENTARY

page 67 *the love that moves the sun and the other stars:* "l'amor che move il sol e l'altre stelle." —Dante Alighieri, *Paradiso,* XXXIII, 145; the last line of *The Divine Comedy.*

page 67 *the vital, immanent, subtle, radiant X:* "The vital, arrogant, fatal, dominant X." —Wallace Stevens, "The Motive for Metaphor."

CHAPTER 34 (Chung Yung, 2)

page 68 *The Master lives in the center:* The center of the universe is the place where you don't believe your own thoughts. From there you can go anywhere.

page 68 *unsatisfied, always / reaching for what is not:* How can they be satisfied if they imagine that there's something lacking? What can possibly fill up that imaginary hole?

page 68 *The Master lives in harmony:* He refuses to join any club that would accept him as a member.

CHAPTER 35 (Chuang-tzu, 13)

page 70 **Huan:** Ruler of the feudal state of Ch'i (r. 685–643 BCE) and the first of five hegemons to dominate China during the Spring and Autumn period (722–481 BCE). He also appears in sections 5, 19, 24, and 29 of the Chuang-tzu. According to the last of these, "In ancient times, Hsiao-po, Duke Huan of Ch'i, murdered his elder brother and married his sister-in-law."

page 70 **was reading a book:** Maybe a precursor of the Tao Te Ching. Maybe, unlike his Danish counterpart, King Claudius, the duke has discovered that murder is self-destructive, and he's genuinely looking for a better way.

page 70 **walked over and said:** He has entered the lion's den. He must really love the duke, since he is willing to risk everything for his enlightenment.

page 70 **The words of the sages:**

> Zen Master Kuei-shan asked his student Yang-shan, "In the forty volumes of the holy Nirvana Sutra, how many words come from the Buddha and how many from demons?"
> Yang-shan said, "They are all demons' words."
> Kuei-shan said, "From now on, no one will be able to pull the wool over your eyes!"

page 70 **they're long dead:** This shows how shallow the duke's reading is. Pien is quick to jump all over it.

page 70 **just the dregs they left behind:** Not only has Pien twisted the lion's tail; he has punched the lion in the nose.

page 70 **How dare you make such a comment:** A predictable response. Not understanding cause and effect, the duke is the slave of his own emotions.

page 70 **Explain yourself, or you die:** In his earlier, hotheaded days, he might not have been so indulgent.

page 70 **Certainly, Your Grace:** Cool as a Chinese cucumber.

page 70 **this place of perfect balance:** What the teaching of the sages is all about.

page 70 **No one taught it to me:** No one can teach it, but they can point the way.

page 70 ***they took their understanding with them:*** Very kind of them, after all.

CHAPTER 36 (Chuang-tzu, 23)

page 72 ***Can you stop looking to others:*** What others? They're all you. Zen Master Lin-chi said, "If you meet the Buddha, kill the Buddha."

page 72 ***Can you return to the beginning of the world:*** It's always now.

COMMENTARY

page 73 ***good and evil:***

> If you want to realize the truth,
> don't be for or against.
> The struggle between good and evil
> is the primal disease of the mind.

—Seng-ts'an

page 73 ***as Jesus implied:*** "Unless you turn around and become like little children, you cannot enter the kingdom of heaven" (Matthew 18:3).

page 73 ***staring... wreath:***

> And the branching of European thought—
> he endured it, like someone who could:
> Rachel stared into the mirror of phenomena,
> and Leah sang and plaited a wreath.

—Osip Mandelstam, poem 293

CHAPTER 37 (Chuang-tzu, 13)

page 74 *her not-doing is the opposite of inaction:* It's the source of intelligent, effortless action.

page 74 *each task does itself, in its own time:* Amazing how those e-mails pile up!

page 74 *as they are, without distortion:* Without the overlay of comparisons or judgments.

CHAPTER 38 (Chuang-tzu, 17)

page 76 *the river Hao:* A small tributary of the Yangtze in Anhui province.

page 76 *Look at the minnows:* Chuang-tzu might have kept his mouth shut. But his comment is just between friends.

page 76 *swimming and leaping:* One can't help but notice.

page 76 *That's what makes fish happy:* If he can't press his friend's buttons, who can?

page 76 *You're not a fish:* A major assumption. But let's not get caught up in details.

page 76 *how do you know:* Now we're getting sidetracked.

page 76 *how do you know that I don't know:* Hmm.

page 76 *True, I'm not you:* Awfully flat-footed. It's not much fun to tweak this fellow.

page 76 **you knew that I knew it:** How sophistical can you get? Come on, Hui-tzu: show some spunk! *Say* something. Anything.

COMMENTARY

page 77 **fire, hail, snow, and frost…reptiles, insects, and birds:** Psalm 148:8–10.

page 77 **joy to the world…you and me:** "Joy to the World," lyrics by Hoyt Axton, performed by Three Dog Night.

CHAPTER 39 (Chuang-tzu, 12)

page 78 **The Master lets go of desire:** Not quite accurate. He desires what is.

page 78 **even the beggars in the street / will benefit from your example:** They won't believe that they shouldn't be beggars in the street, for now. This will save them a lot of grief and guilt.

page 78 **He perfects the whole world in his heart:** He realizes that his heart contains the whole world.

page 78 **are strung on a single thread:** We can call that thread "mind."

CHAPTER 40 (Chuang-tzu, 14)

page 80 **What, without any effort, / makes everything happen:** It just happens. Amazing.

page 80 **Do things just happen to turn out / exactly the way they do?:** Yes—luckily for us.

page 80 **stirs up this unfathomable joy?:**

To know that what is impenetrable to us really exists and manifests itself as the highest wisdom and the most radiant beauty, which our dull senses can grasp only in their most primitive forms—this knowledge, this feeling, is the essence of true religiousness. My religion consists in a humble awe before the higher reality that reveals itself in the smallest details that we are able to perceive with our weak, fragile minds. The deep conviction that there is a superior intelligence, whose power reveals itself in the immeasurable universe, forms my idea of God.

—Albert Einstein

COMMENTARY

page 81 **the motivators for right action:**

I've heard people say that they cling to their painful thoughts because they're afraid that without them they wouldn't be activists for peace. "If I felt completely peaceful," they say, "why would I bother taking action at all?" My answer is "Because that's what love does." To think that we need sadness or outrage to motivate us to do what's right is insane. As if the clearer and happier you get, the less kind you become. As if when someone finds freedom, she just sits around all day with drool running down her chin. My experience is the opposite. Love is action. It's clear, it's kind, it's effortless, and it's irresistible.

—Byron Katie, *A Thousand Names for Joy*

CHAPTER 41 (Chuang-tzu, 12, 25)

page 82 **All things return to it:** That's how it seems. But they never left. They were never "they."

page 82 **The Tao is beyond words:**

> Where can I find someone
> who has penetrated beyond words?
> That's whom I'd like to have a word with.
>
> —Chuang-tzu, 26

page 82 **Only when you are truly / unattached to words or to silence:** Only when you realize that every word out of your mouth is a lie.

page 82 **can you express the truth:** And not even then.

CHAPTER 42 (Chuang-tzu, 17)

page 84 **the river P'u:** It flows from the northern end of Shantung province into Shanghai.

page 84 **arrived:** They had asked in town. Everyone knew where to find him.

page 84 **Ch'u:** A kingdom in southern China during the Spring and Autumn (722–481 BCE) and Warring States (481–212 BCE) periods. At the height of its power, the Ch'u empire occupied the present-day provinces of Hunan, Hupei, Ch'ung-ch'ing, Honan, Shanghai, and parts of Kiangsu.

page 84 **The king requests:** Most kings would have said, "I demand…" If this king means what he says, he is a truly courteous man.

page 84 **there is a sacred tortoise:** More accurately, there *was* a tortoise.

There *is* just his shell. Too slow to escape the trappers, he obviously wasn't an ancestor of the tortoise who outran Achilles.

page 84 **wrapped in silk and encased in a golden box:** Just like the king himself.

page 84 **if you were this tortoise:** There can be only one answer (unless you're a politician).

page 84 **The latter, certainly:** These officials are honest men.

page 84 **Give my compliments to His Majesty:** "I can't truthfully say that this is a great honor, but I mean no offense."

page 84 **I am happy right here, crawling around in the mud:** "This small life is enough for me. And maybe there will be grilled trout for dinner."

CHAPTER 43 (Chuang-tzu, 20)

page 86 **Give up wanting to be important:** That tree I planted a while back in the village of Nothingness—it must be huge by now.

page 86 **let your footsteps leave no trace:** Even if you let them leave a trace, they don't.

page 86 **the land of the great silence:** Ahhh.

page 86 **Realize that all boats are empty:** Once you take total responsibility for your life, you understand that no one is the doer.

page 86 **and nothing can possibly offend you:** There's no you left to be offended.

COMMENTARY

page 87 **If you're offended:** "If you're not offended, you're not paying attention." (Bumper sticker noticed in Santa Monica.) A clearer statement (you'd need a wider bumper or a smaller font) would be: "If you don't notice that greed, hatred, and ignorance cause great suffering in the world, and if you're not moved to end the suffering, you're not paying attention."

CHAPTER 44 (Chuang-tzu, 14)

page 88 **trying to be benevolent:** It's the trying that is the problem, not the benevolence.

page 88 **you must move with the freedom of the wind:** Without a goal or purpose.

COMMENTARY

page 89 **Lao-tzu says:**

> Throw away holiness and wisdom,
> and people will be a hundred times happier.
> Throw away morality and justice,
> and people will do the right thing.
>
> —Tao Te Ching, 19

page 89 **till the right action arises by itself:**

> Do you have the patience to wait
> till your mud settles and the water is clear?
> Can you remain unmoving
> till the right action arises by itself?
>
> —Tao Te Ching, 15

CHAPTER 45 (Chuang-tzu, 17)

*page 90 **You can't reach for the positive:*** Reaching for it means that you think it's somewhere else.

*page 90 **The Master stands beyond opposites:*** By including them. There is no quality, good or bad, that she can't easily find in herself.

COMMENTARY

*page 91 **The tree that moves some:*** William Blake, Letter to Rev. Dr. Trusler, August 23, 1799.

*page 91 **Archimedes** (287–212 BCE):* Quoted by Pappus of Alexandria in *Synagoge*, Book VIII, c. 340 CE.

CHAPTER 46 (Chuang-tzu, 19)

*page 92 **Ch'ing:*** The *Tso chuan*, China's oldest narrative history, mentions him under the fourth year of Duke Hsiang (569 BCE). (Watson's note.)

*page 92 **Lu:*** Confucius' home province, which covered the central and southwest regions of modern Shantung province. It was annexed by the state of Ch'u in 256 BCE.

*page 92 **How did your art achieve something of such unearthly beauty?:*** A more effusive version of Prince Wen-hui's question to his cook in chapter 14.

*page 92 **I don't know anything about art:*** It's not what I do; it's who I am.

*page 92 **I harmonize inner and outer:*** With no distractions, I become fully myself.

CHAPTER 47 (Chuang-tzu, 17)

page 94 ***You can't talk about the Tao / with a person who thinks he knows something:*** You also can't talk about it with a person who knows he knows nothing.

page 94 ***beyond the limits of yourself:*** Beyond what you think is true.

CHAPTER 48 (Chuang-tzu, 33)

page 96 ***as though you didn't exist:*** As though you were a cheerful revenant in your own life.

page 96 ***there is nothing to oppose:*** In a sweet reverse megalomania, you realize that because there's no you, everything in the universe exists for your sake alone.

COMMENTARY

page 97 ***Why do the wicked prosper?:*** Jeremiah 12:1.

CHAPTER 49 (Chuang-tzu, 19)

page 98 ***Chi Hsing-tzu was training a gamecock:*** His job may be difficult, but compared to a monkey trainer's it's a piece of cake.

page 98 ***for the king:*** We are told neither the king's name nor his country. He has become His Generic Majesty, a mere prop in the story, a fragment of his own impatience.

page 98 ***the king asked:*** As a student of animal (and thus human) nature? Or is he merely interested in having the best gamecock in the neighborhood?

page 98 **always ready to pick a fight:** Fighting is not what he's being trained for.

page 98 **He still becomes excited when a rival bird appears:** It's always yourself you face. The thought of an other is a distraction.

page 98 **He still gets an angry glint in his eye:** What a meticulous eye Chi must have!

page 98 **he doesn't react:** He no longer has a sense of competition. There's no interest in being the alpha male.

page 98 **His focus is inside:** He has learned not to rely on his own strength. You could say that this is total self-confidence, but actually it's confidence in what is beyond the self.

page 98 **Other birds will take one look at him and run:** The aggressive ones, that is. The ones who don't have anything to prove will simply go about their business.

COMMENTARY

page 99 **discretion:** "The better part of valour is discretion; in the which better part I have saved my life." Falstaff, in *Henry IV, Part 1*, V.iv.

CHAPTER 50 (Chung Yung, 14)

page 100 **he turns around:** After all, it's not the bow's fault.

page 100 **and seeks / the reason for his failure in himself:** It's fascinating to be your own student. As Shunryu Suzuki Rōshi (1904–1971) used to say, "Everything's perfect, but there's a lot of room for improvement."

CHAPTER 51 (Chuang-tzu, 20)

page 102 **Unchain yourself from achievement:** Question all thoughts of achievement, which chain you to an identity.

page 102 **unhindered, / unnoticed, unnamed:** Just doing what you do, without needing anyone's approval.

COMMENTARY

page 103 **are but as yesterday:** "For a thousand years in thy sight are but as yesterday when it is past." —Psalm 90:4 (King James Version).

page 103 **Eternity laughs:** "Eternity is in love with the productions of time." —William Blake, *The Marriage of Heaven and Hell.*

page 103 **the lone and level sands:**

> Nothing beside remains. Round the decay
> Of that colossal wreck, boundless and bare,
> The lone and level sands stretch far away.
>
> —Percy Bysshe Shelley, "Ozymandias"

page 103 **Everyday mind is the Tao:**

> Chao-chou asked Zen Master Nan-ch'üan, "What is the Tao?"
> Nan-ch'üan said, "Everyday mind is the Tao."
> Chao-chou said, "How can I approach it?"
> Nan-ch'üan said, "If you try to approach it, you'll miss it."
> "But if I don't approach it, how can I understand it?"

Nan-ch'üan said, "It's not a question of understanding or not understanding. Understanding is
delusion; not understanding is indifference. But
when you reach the unattainable Tao, it is like pure
space, limitless and serene. Where is there room in
it for yes or no?"

CHAPTER 52 (Chuang-tzu, 8)

page 104 **Do you think that you know what's best?**: "I know" is the song
of the sirens. If your ears aren't stopped, lash yourself to the mast.

page 104 **should conform to your way of thinking:** This kind of
benevolence is one of the subtle disguises of the ego. It's
compassion's beady-eyed twin.

COMMENTARY

page 105 **In order to make an omelet, you [have] to crack a few eggs:**
This statement is said to have originated with Maximilien de
Robespierre (1758–1794).

CHAPTER 53 (Chuang-tzu, 18)

page 106 **Lieh-tzu** (Master Lieh, a.k.a. Lieh Yü-k'ou; c. 450–c. 375
BCE): Traditionally known as the third Taoist sage, after Lao-tzu
and Chuang-tzu. The (very dull) Book of Lieh-tzu, ascribed to
him, actually dates from around 300 CE. He appears as a character
in sections 1, 7, 18, 19, 21, 28, and 32 of the Chuang-tzu.

page 106 **saw an old skull:** Nothing himself, like Wallace Stevens'
Snow Man, Lieh-tzu beholds "nothing that is not there and the
nothing that is."

Zen Master Tao-wu paid a visit to his brother-monk Zen Master Yün-yen, who was very sick. "Where can I meet you again," he said, "if you die and leave only your corpse here?"

Yün-yen said, "I'll meet you in the place where nothing is born and nothing dies."

Tao-wu said, "That answer is okay. But what you should have said is that there's no place where nothing is born and nothing dies, and that we don't need to meet each other again."

CHAPTER 54 (Chung Yung, 12)

page 108 the Tao begins in the relation:

Once we begin to question our thoughts, our partners, alive, dead, or divorced, are always our greatest teachers. There's no mistake about the person you're with; he or she is the perfect teacher for you, whether or not the relationship works out, and once you enter inquiry, you come to see that clearly. There's never a mistake in the universe. So if your partner is angry, good. If there are things about him that you consider flaws, good, because these flaws are your own, you're projecting them, and you can write them down, inquire, and set yourself free. People go to India to find a guru, but you don't have to: You're living with one. Your partner will give you everything you need for your own freedom.

—Byron Katie, *I Need Your Love—Is That True?*

page 108 between man and woman: It may also begin in the relation between man and man, and between woman and woman.

CHAPTER 55 (Chuang-tzu, 22)

page 110 *Who can understand / how the two are related?:*

> It is strange that people don't want to know about
> the present, whose existence nobody can doubt,
> but are always eager to know about the past or the
> future, both of which are unknown. What is birth
> and what is death? Why go to birth and death to
> understand what you experience every day in sleep-
> ing and waking? When you sleep, this body and the
> world do not exist for you, and these questions do
> not worry you, and yet you exist, the same you that
> exists now while waking. It is only when you wake
> up that you have a body and see the world. If you
> understand waking and sleep properly, you will
> understand life and death. But waking and sleeping
> happen every day, so people don't notice the won-
> der of it, but only want to know about birth and
> death.
>
> —Ramana Maharshi

page 110 **to understand the one breath:** The exhalation is not opposed
to the inhalation.

CHAPTER 56 (Chuang-tzu, 21)

page 112 **looked ordinary:**

> Zen Master Hsueh-feng asked a monk where he
> came from. The monk said, "From the Monastery
> of Spiritual Light."
> Hsueh-feng said, "In the daytime, sunlight; in
> the evening, lamplight. What is spiritual light?"
> The monk couldn't answer.

Hsueh-feng answered for him: "Sunlight. Lamp-light."

page 112 ***The more they gave to others:***

The supreme perfection of giving consists in the threefold purity. What is the threefold purity? When a bodhisattva gives a gift, he doesn't perceive a self who gives, or a self who receives, or a gift, nor does he perceive a reward for his giving. He surrenders that gift to all beings, but he perceives neither beings nor self. He dedicates that gift to enlightenment, but he doesn't perceive any such thing as enlightenment.

—*The Perfection of Wisdom Sutra in 25,000 Lines*
(c. 2nd–4th century CE)

CHAPTER 57 (Chuang-tzu, 18)

page 114 ***the Marquis of Lu:*** Because such a blockhead couldn't have asked the delicate question in chapter 46, I presume that this marquis was an ancestor or descendant of the other one.

page 114 ***his ancestral temple:*** Where the prejudices and superstitions of a hundred generations were enshrined. Undoubtedly, there was a sacred tortoise as well, wrapped in silk and encased in a golden box.

page 114 ***the bird became dazed:*** At the extent of human selfishness and stupidity.

page 114 ***In three days it was dead:*** A sensible exit strategy. Requiescat in pace.

page 114 ***as the marquis would have liked to be treated:*** The point of

Jesus' statement is empathy ("Whatever you want others to do to you, do to them. This is the essence of the Law and the prophets." Matthew 7:12). But when the mind is confused, doing to others what you would want done to you can be deadly. The Chung Yung's so-called negative form of the Golden Rule ("Don't do to others what you wouldn't want done to you"; see chapter 24) may be more useful. It was stated as early as Confucius' *Analects* (c. 500 BCE), and five centuries later by Hillel the Elder (c. 40 BCE– 10 CE). When a Gentile asked him to summarize the Law, Hillel said, "What you yourself hate, don't do to your neighbor. This is the whole Law; the rest is commentary. Go now and learn."

page 114 **feed on mudfish and minnows:** Those happy minnows wouldn't even know what hit them. Their death would be instantaneous and carefree, like their life.

COMMENTARY

page 115 **the golden fool:**

> He has observed the golden rule
> Till he's become the golden fool.
>
> —William Blake

page 115 **with his glittering eye:**

> He holds him with his glittering eye—
> The Wedding-Guest stood still,
> And listens like a three years' child:
> The Mariner hath his will.
>
> —Samuel Taylor Coleridge,
> "The Rime of the Ancient Mariner"

page 115 **Love your neighbor as yourself:** Leviticus 19:18.

CHAPTER 58 (Chuang-tzu, 19)

page 116 ***the way he falls is different:*** He's not tensed up, bracing himself against a future.

COMMENTARY

page 117 ***the road of excess:*** "The road of excess leads to the palace of wisdom." —William Blake, *The Marriage of Heaven and Hell*. This can be true as well.

CHAPTER 59 (Chuang-tzu, 22)

page 118 ***you will realize how simple life is:*** Life is mind projected. If it's simple here, it's simple there.

page 118 ***looking for impossible answers:*** The answers are impossible to find outside you.

COMMENTARY

page 119 ***Simplify, simplify:*** Henry David Thoreau, *Walden*.

page 119 ***a word to the wise is sufficient:*** From the Latin proverb *verbum sat sapienti*.

CHAPTER 60 (Chuang-tzu, 24)

page 120 ***it doesn't seek perfection:*** How would it even know what perfection is?

page 120 ***You return to yourself:*** To the source.

COMMENTARY

page 121 **This is perfect... the remainder is perfect:** The invocation to the Isha Upanishad, in *The Ten Principal Upanishads*, trans. W. B. Yeats and Shree Purohit Swami.

page 121 **The unattainable—how close it is!:** Osip Mandelstam, poem 278.

CHAPTER 61 (Chuang-tzu, 18)

page 122 **came to offer his condolences:** He still doesn't get it.

page 122 **pounding on a tub:** Singing the Taoist version of "O Sole Mio," which is in a major key.

page 122 **don't you owe her a few tears:** Tears would be disrespectful.

page 122 **that's a bit much, don't you think?:** It's just enough.

page 122 **I mourned as anyone else would:** Love will go to any length for the sake of a friend. Zen Master Yang-shan (814–890) once said, "In my shop I handle all kinds of merchandise. If someone comes looking for rat shit, I'll sell him rat shit. If someone comes looking for gold, I'll sell him pure gold."

page 122 **before she had a soul:** Any form of separate identity.

page 122 **lying at peace in her vast room:** Having everything I could ever want for her.

page 122 **So I stopped:** End of little morality tale. Exit. Polite applause.

CHAPTER 62 (Chuang-tzu, 12)

page 124 or pays special attention / to the lovely, the virtuous, or the wise: Do fish pay special attention to water? When you're in harmony with the way things are, you see that all of us are beautiful in our own way, all of us are innately wise, and as virtuous as we can possibly be, given the thoughts we're believing.

page 124 They keep no records of their good deeds: There are poets, artists, and musicians, but no biographers or historians.

page 124 all their actions / have vanished, without a trace: Like everything else. But the *effects* of their actions keep filling their descendants with gratitude.

COMMENTARY

page 125 Dr. Johnson: Boswell's *The Life of Samuel Johnson, LLD*, April 13, 1778.

page 125 Yeats: In his poem "The Tower." The girl's name was Mary Hynes. Actually, it was because her beauty had been praised by the poet Raftery that the farmers jostled to see her, "so great a glory did the song confer."

CHAPTER 63 (Chung Yung, 33)

page 126 Though the fish sinks to the bottom: Those bottom-feeding thoughts—they're the craftiest.

page 126 before it can do any harm: If there's discord, it's already doing harm.

COMMENTARY

page 127 **When a pickpocket sees a saint, he sees only his pockets:** This saying has been attributed to Ramakrishna (1836–1886).

CHAPTER 64 (Chung Yung, 20, 25)

page 128 **we become truly human:** That is to say, free.

page 128 **when we fulfill all beings:** We can't help fulfilling them, because their nature is exactly the same as ours.

page 128 **everything we do is right:**

> There's no mistake, and there's nothing lacking. We're always going to get what we need, not what we *think* we need. Then we come to see that what we need is not only what we have, it's what we want. Then we come to want only what is. That way we always succeed, whatever happens.
> —Byron Katie, *A Thousand Names for Joy*

NOTES ON THE ADAPTATION

In the interest of transparency, I have appended scholarly translations of the passages where my adaptation has been particularly free, along with a few acknowledgments and confessions. (The Chuang-tzu passages are translated by Burton Watson, unless otherwise indicated.)

CHAPTER 3

"The Great Way is not named; Great Discriminations are not spoken; Great Benevolence is not benevolent; Great Modesty is not humble; Great Daring does not attack. If the Way is made clear, it is not the Way. If discriminations are put into words, they do not suffice. If benevolence has a constant object, it cannot be universal. If modesty is fastidious, it cannot be trusted. If daring attacks, it cannot be complete. These five are all round, but they tend toward the square.

"Therefore understanding that rests in what it does not understand is the finest. Who can understand discriminations that are not spoken, the Way that is not a way? If he can understand this, he may be called the Reservoir of Heaven. Pour into it and it is never full, dip from it and it never runs dry, and yet it does not know where the supply comes from. This is called the Shaded Light."

CHAPTER 4

clinging to a particular side of reality without realizing the underlying oneness: I have followed Merton's interpretation here: "stubbornly clinging to one partial view of things, refusing to see a deeper agreement between this and its complementary opposite…" Watson: "trying to make things into one without realizing that they are all the same…"

simply knew how to adapt to reality, and he lost nothing by it: Here again, I have followed Merton: "had been willing to change his personal arrangement in order to meet objective conditions. He lost nothing by it!" Watson: "Let them, if they want to."

CHAPTER 5

The Master understands / that there is nothing to understand: I have added these last two lines, just in case.

CHAPTER 6

The Master is not trapped in opposites… beside the point: "Therefore the sage does not proceed in such a way, but illuminates all in the light of Heaven. He too recognizes a 'this,' but a 'this' which is also 'that,' a 'that' which is also 'this.' His 'that' has both a right and a wrong in it; his 'this' too has both a right and a wrong in it. So, in fact, does he still have a 'this' and 'that'? Or does he in fact no longer have a 'this' and 'that'?"

When we find this pivot...endlessly: I have followed Merton here: "When the wise man grasps this pivot, he is in the center of the circle, and there he stands while 'Yes' and 'No' pursue each other around the circumference." Literally, the passage reads: "When the pivot is located at the center of the circle, it can respond infinitely, both to what is and to what isn't. Hence the saying 'There is nothing like clarity.'"

CHAPTER 8

forgotten the way back: I have omitted the following lovely passage, which didn't tend itself to verse. Literally: "Lady Li was the daughter of the guard on the frontier of Ai. When she was first taken captive by the Chin army, she wept until her robe was drenched with tears. But once she went to live in the king's palace, shared his bed, and ate the magnificent food on his table, she wondered why she had ever wept."

all this was one big dream: I have omitted the next passage except for one sentence. "Yet the stupid believe they are awake, busily and brightly assuming they understand things, calling this man ruler, that one herdsman—how dense! Confucius and you are both dreaming! And when I say you are dreaming, I am dreaming, too. Words like these will be labeled the Supreme Swindle. Yet, after ten thousand generations, a great sage may appear who will know their meaning, and it will still be as though he appeared with astonishing speed."

CHAPTER 11

First stanza: I have omitted the following: "Chu Ch'ueh-tzu said to Chang Wu-tzu, 'I have heard Confucius say that the sage...'"

amid the world's dust and grime: I have omitted the passage that follows this. [Chu Ch'ueh-tzu said,] "'Confucius himself regarded these as wild and flippant words, though I believe they describe the working of the mysterious Way. What do you think of them?' Chang Wu-tzu said, 'Even the Yellow Emperor would be confused if he heard such words, so how could you expect Confucius to understand them? What's more, you're too hasty in your own appraisal. You see an egg and demand a crowing cock, see a crossbow pellet and demand a roast dove. I'm going to try speaking some reckless words and I want you to listen to them recklessly. How will that be?'"

She lets the confused stay confused...different from what it is: "...'leaves the confusion and muddle as it is, and looks on slaves as exalted. Ordinary men strain and struggle; the sage is stupid and blockish. He takes part in ten thousand ages and achieves simplicity in oneness. For him, all the ten thousand things are what they are, and thus they enfold each other.'"

CHAPTER 12

Heaven is a bright emptiness...manifold splendor: "The heaven appearing before us is only this bright shining mass; but in its immeasurable extent, the sun, the moon, stars and constellations are suspended in it, and all things are embraced under it. The earth, appearing before us, is but a handful of soil; but in all its breadth and depth, it sustains mighty mountains without feeling their weight; rivers and seas dash against it without causing it to leak. The mountain appearing before us is only a mass of rock; but in all the vastness of its size, grass and vegetation grow upon it, birds and beasts dwell on it, and treasures of precious minerals are found in it. The water appearing before us is but a ladleful of liquid; but in all its unfathomable depths, the largest crustaceans, dragons, fishes, and turtles, are produced in them, and all useful products abound in them."—Ku Hungming

CHAPTER 13

"What is acceptable we call acceptable; what is unacceptable we call unacceptable. A road is made by people walking on it; things are so because they are called so. What makes them so? Making them so makes them so. What makes them not so? Making them not so makes them not so. Things all must have that which is so; things all must have that which is acceptable. There is nothing that is not so, nothing that is not acceptable.

"For this reason, whether you point to a little stalk or a great pillar, a leper or the beautiful Hsi-shih, things ribald and shady or things grotesque and strange, the Way makes them all into one. Their dividedness is their completeness; their completeness is their impairment. No thing is either complete or impaired, but all are made into one again. Only the man of far-reaching vision knows how to make them into one. So he has no use [for categories], but relegates all to the constant. The constant is the useful; the useful is the passable; the passable is the successful; and with success, all is accomplished. He relies upon this alone, relies upon it and does not know he is doing so. This is called the Way."

CHAPTER 14

not with my eyes: I have omitted the following sentence: "Perception and understanding have come to a stop, and spirit moves where it wants."

more than enough room for it: I have omitted the following sentence: "That's why after nineteen years the blade of my knife is still as good as when it first came from the grindstone."

the flesh falls apart on its own: I have omitted the following phrase: "...like a clod of earth crumbling to the ground."

let the joy of the work: I have borrowed this phrase from Merton.

CHAPTER 15

Their breath went deep: This line is followed by a passage that, according to A. C. Graham, may be a gloss by a later scholiast: "The Master [literally, 'the Genuine Man'] breathes from the heels; ordinary men breathe from the throat. Crushed and submissive, they gasp out words as if they were retching. Where passions and desires are deep, the spiritual impulse is shallow."

CHAPTER 16

Consider a window... the whole world is filled with light: I have followed Merton here: "Look at this window: it is nothing but a hole in the wall, but because of it the whole room is full of light. So when the faculties are empty, the heart is full of light." Watson: "Look into that closed room, the empty chamber where brightness is born!"

CHAPTER 17

Second stanza: "'... Therefore, they should not be enough to destroy your harmony; they should not be allowed to enter the Spirit Storehouse. If you can harmonize and delight in them, master them and never be at a loss for joy, if you can do this day and night without break and make it be spring with everything, mingling with all and creating the moment within your own mind—this is what I call being whole in power.'

[Duke Ai said,] 'What do you mean when you say his virtue takes no form?'

[Confucius said,] 'Among level things, water at rest is the most perfect, and therefore it can serve as a standard. It guards what is inside and shows no movement outside.'"

"Nan-po Tzu-k'uei said to the Woman Crookback, 'You are old in years and yet your complexion is that of a child. Why is this?'

'I have heard the Way!'

'Can the Way be learned?' asked Nan-po Tzu-k'uei.

'Goodness, how could that be? Anyway, you aren't the man to do it. Now there's Pu-liang Yi—he has the talent of a sage but not the Way of a sage, whereas I have the Way of a sage but not the talent of a sage. I thought I would try to teach him and see if I could really get anywhere near to making him a sage. It's easier to explain the Way of a sage to someone who has the talent of a sage, you know. So I began explaining and kept him at it for three days, and after that he was able to put the world outside himself. When he had put the world outside himself, I kept at him for seven days more, and after that he was able to put things outside himself. When he had put things outside himself, I kept at him for nine days more, and after that he was able to put life outside himself. After he had put life outside himself, he was able to achieve the brightness of dawn, and when he had achieved the brightness of dawn, he could see his own aloneness. After he had managed to see his own aloneness, he could do away with past and present, and after he had done away with past and present, he was able to enter where there is no life and no death. That which kills life does not die; that which gives life to life does not live. This is the kind of thing it is: there's nothing it doesn't send off, nothing it doesn't welcome, nothing it doesn't destroy, nothing it doesn't complete.'"

They scaled the heights, never dizzy . . . embodied the Tao: "A man like this could climb the high places and not be frightened, could enter the water and not get wet, could enter the fire and not get burned. His knowledge was able to climb all the way up to the Way like this."

CHAPTER 21

"…Confucius said, 'Life and death are great affairs, and yet they are no change to him. Though heaven and earth flop over and fall down, it is no loss to him. He sees clearly into what has no falsehood and does not shift with things. He takes it as fate that things should change and he holds fast to the source.'"

CHAPTER 22

"You have had the audacity to take on human form and you are delighted. But the human form has ten thousand changes that never come to an end. Your joys, then, must be uncountable. Therefore, the sage wanders in the realm where things cannot get away from him, and all are preserved. He delights in early death; he delights in old age; he delights in the beginning; he delights in the end. If he can serve as a model for men, how much more so that which the ten thousand things are tied to and all changes alike wait upon!"

CHAPTER 23

looked at one another and smiled: I have omitted the following sentence: "There was no disagreement in their hearts and so the four of them became friends."

my neck bones point to the sky: I have omitted the following sentence: "'It must be some dislocation of the yin and yang!'"

Anyone who understands the proper order of things . . . no complaint whatsoever: "Be content with this time and dwell in this order and then neither sorrow nor joy can touch you. In ancient times this was called the 'freeing of the bound.' There are those who cannot free themselves, because they are bound by things. But nothing can ever win against Heaven—that's the way it's always been. What would I have to resent?"

CHAPTER 25

When speaking to people . . . isn't really itself: I have added these lines. Literally, the entire passage reads: "To use a finger to show that a finger is not a finger is not as good as using a non-finger to show that a finger is not a finger. To use a horse to show that a horse is not a horse is not as good as using a non-horse to show that a horst is not a horse. Heaven and earth are one finger; the ten thousand things are one horse."

CHAPTER 27

My dialogue is a variation on the original theme.

"Penumbra said to Shadow, 'A little while ago you were walking and now you're standing still; a little while ago you were sitting and now you're standing up. Why this lack of independent action?'

"Shadow said, 'Do I have to wait for something before I can be like this? Does what I wait for also have to wait for something before it can be like this? Am I waiting for the scales of a snake or the wings of a cicada? How do I know why it is so? How do I know why it isn't so?'"

CHAPTER 28

"Do not be an embodier of fame; do not be a storehouse of schemes; do not be an undertaker of projects; do not be a proprietor of wisdom.

Embody to the fullest what has no end and wander where there is no trail. Hold on to all that you have received from Heaven but do not think you have gotten anything. Be empty, that is all. The Perfect Man uses his mind like a mirror—going after nothing, welcoming nothing, responding but not storing. Therefore he can win out over things and not hurt himself."

CHAPTER 29

Literally: "If there is no other, there is no I. If there is no I, there is nothing to perceive an other. This is close to the meaning. But I don't know what causes it to be that way. It seems as though there is a True Lord, but there is no evidence for him. Certainly he acts, but I can't see his form. He has identity but no form."

CHAPTER 31

Another variation on a theme by Chuang-tzu. (I have added the checkers.)

"Hui Tzu said to Chuang Tzu, 'Can a man really be without feelings?'

"Chuang Tzu: 'Yes.'

"Hui Tzu: 'But a man who has no feelings—how can you call him a man?'

"Chuang Tzu: 'The Way gave him a face; Heaven gave him a form—why can't you call him a man?'

"Hui Tzu: 'But if you've already called him a man, how can he be without feelings?'

"Chuang Tzu: 'That's not what I mean by feelings. When I talk about having no feelings, I mean that a man doesn't allow likes or dislikes to get in and do him harm. He just lets things be the way they are and doesn't try to help life along.'

"Hui Tzu: 'If he doesn't try to help life along, then how can he keep himself alive?'

"Chuang Tzu: 'The Way gave him a face; Heaven gave him a form. He doesn't let likes or dislikes get in and do him harm. You, now—you treat your spirit like an outsider. You wear out your energy, leaning on a tree and moaning, slumping at your desk and dozing—Heaven picked out a body for you and you use it to gibber about "hard" and "white"!'"

CHAPTER 33

I have added the second stanza.

CHAPTER 36

"...Lao Tzu said, 'Ah—the basic rule of life-preservation. Can you embrace the One? Can you keep from losing it? Can you, without tortoise shell or divining stalks, foretell fortune and misfortune? Do you know where to stop, do you know where to leave off? Do you know how to disregard it in others and instead look for it in yourself? Can you be brisk and unflagging? Can you be rude and unwitting? Can you be a little baby? The baby howls all day, yet its throat never gets hoarse—harmony at its height! The baby makes fists all day, yet its fingers never get cramped—virtue is all it holds to. The baby stares all day without blinking its eyes—it has no preferences in the world of externals. To move without knowing where you are going, to sit at home without knowing what you are doing, traipsing and trailing about with other things, riding along with them on the same wave—this is the basic rule of life-preservation, this and nothing more.'"

CHAPTER 37

"The sage is still not because he takes stillness to be good and therefore is still. The ten thousand things are insufficient to distract his mind—that is the reason he is still. Water that is still gives back a clear image of beard and eyebrows; reposing in the water level, it offers a measure to the great carpenter. And if water in stillness possesses such clarity, how much more must pure spirit. The sage's mind in stillness is the mirror of Heaven and earth, the glass of the ten thousand things."

CHAPTER 39

"The Master said: 'The Way covers and bears up the ten thousand things—vast, vast is its greatness! The gentleman must pluck out his mind! To act through inaction is called Heaven. To speak through inaction is called Virtue. To love men and bring profit to things is called benevolence. To make the unlike alike is called magnitude. To move beyond barrier and distinction is called liberality. To possess the ten thousand unlikes is called wealth. To hold fast to Virtue is called enrootment. To mature in Virtue is called establishment. To follow the Way is called completion. To see that external things do not blunt the will is called perfection. When the gentleman clearly comprehends these ten things, then how huge will be the greatness of his mind setting forth, how endless his ramblings with the ten thousand things!

"'Such a man will leave the gold hidden in the mountains, the pearls hidden in the depths. He will see no profit in money and goods, no enticement in eminence and wealth, no joy in long life, no grief in early death, no honor in affluence, no shame in poverty. He will not snatch the profits of a whole generation and make them his private hoard; he will not lord it over the world and think that he dwells in glory. His glory is enlightenment, [for he knows that] the ten thousand things belong to one storehouse, that life and death share the same body.'"

CHAPTER 40

I have added the first two lines.

CHAPTER 41

Because it is without form... express the truth: "...[Great Imperial Accord said,] 'While there are names and realities, you are in the presence of things. When there are no names and realities, you exist in the absence of things. You can talk about it, you can think about it; but the more you talk about it, the farther away you get from it....

"'The Way cannot be thought of as being, nor can it be thought of as non-being. In calling it the Way we are only adopting a temporary expedient. 'Nothing does it,' 'something makes it like this'—these occupy a mere corner of the realm of things. What connection could they have with the Great Method? If you talk in a worthy manner, you can talk all day long and all of it will pertain to the Way. But if you talk in an unworthy manner, you can talk all day long and all of it will pertain to mere things. The perfection of the Way and things—neither words nor silence are worthy of expressing it. Not to talk, not to be silent—this is the highest form of debate.'"

CHAPTER 43

First stanza: "...[The Master from south of the Market said,] 'He who possesses men will know hardship; he who is possessed by men will know care. Therefore Yao neither possessed men nor allowed himself to be possessed by them. So I ask you to rid yourself of hardship, to cast off your cares, and to wander alone with the Way to the Land of Great Silence.'"

CHAPTER 45

"...[Jo of the North Sea said,] 'From the point of view of function, if we regard a thing as useful because there is a certain usefulness to it, then among all the ten thousand things there are none that are not useful. If we regard a thing as useless because there is a certain uselessness to it, then among the ten thousand things there are none that are not useless. If we know that east and west are mutually opposed but that one cannot do without the other, then we can estimate the degree of function.

"'From the point of view of preference, if we regard a thing as right because there is a certain right to it, then among the ten thousand things there are none that are not right. If we regard a thing as wrong because there is a certain wrong to it, then among the ten thousand things there are none that are not wrong. If we know that Yao and Chieh each thought himself right and condemned the other as wrong, then we may understand how there are preferences in behavior.

"'In ancient times Yao abdicated in favor of Shun and Shun ruled as emperor; K'uai abdicated in favor of Chih and Chih was destroyed. T'ang and Wu fought and became kings; Duke Po fought and was wiped out. Looking at it this way, we see that struggling or giving way, behaving like a Yao or like a Chieh, may be at one time noble and at another time mean. It is impossible to establish any constant rule.

"'A beam or pillar can be used to batter down a city wall, but it is no good for stopping up a little hole—this refers to a difference in function. Thoroughbreds like Ch'i-chi and Hua-liu could gallop a thousand li in one day, but when it came to catching rats they were no match for the wildcat or the weasel—this refers to a difference in skill. The horned owl catches fleas at night and can spot the tip of a hair, but when daylight comes, no matter how wide it opens its eyes, it cannot see a mound or a hill—this refers to a difference in nature. Now do you say, that you are going to make Right your master and do away with Wrong, or make Order your master and do away with Disorder? If you do, then you have not understood the principle of heaven and earth or the nature of the ten thousand things.' "

CHAPTER 46

identified with a body: I have omitted the sentence that follows: "By that time, the ruler and his court no longer exist for me."

all I have to do is get started: I have omitted the phrase that follows: "if not, I let it go."

CHAPTER 48

"The Barrier Keeper Yin said, 'When a man does not dwell in self, then things will of themselves reveal their forms to him. His movement is like that of water, his stillness like that of a mirror, his responses like those of an echo. Blank-eyed, he seems to be lost; motionless, he has the limpidity of water. Because he is one with it, he achieves harmony; should he reach out for it, he would lose it. Never does he go ahead of other men, but always follows in their wake.' "

CHAPTER 51

"...[T'ai-kung Jen said,] 'I have heard the Man of Great Completion say: "Boasts are a sign of no success; success once won faces overthrow; fame once won faces ruin." Who can rid himself of success and fame, return and join the common run of men? His Way flows abroad, but he does not rest in brightness; his Virtue moves, but he does not dwell in fame. Vacant, addled, he seems close to madness. Wiping out his footprints, sloughing off his power, he does not work for success or fame. So he has no cause to blame other men, nor other men to blame him. The Perfect Man wants no repute. Why then do you delight in it so?'"

CHAPTER 52

"He who holds to True Rightness does not lose the original form of his inborn nature. So for him joined things are not webbed toes, things forking off are not superfluous fingers, the long is never too much, the short is never too little. The duck's legs are short, but to stretch them out would worry him; the crane's legs are long, but to cut them down would make him sad. What is long by nature needs no cutting off; what is short by nature needs no stretching. That would be no way to get rid of worry. I wonder, then, if benevolence and righteousness are part of man's true form? Those benevolent men—how much worrying they do!"

CHAPTER 53

there is no such thing as death and no such thing as life: I have omitted the following two sentences: "Are you really unhappy? Am I really enjoying myself?"

CHAPTER 56

"...Confucius, hearing of the incident, said, 'He was a True Man of old, the kind that the wise cannot argue with, the beautiful cannot seduce, the violent cannot intimidate; even Fu Hsi or the Yellow Emperor could not have befriended him. Life and death are great affairs, and yet they are no change to him—how much less to him are things like titles and stipends! With such a man, his spirit may soar over Mount T'ai without hindrance, may plunge into the deepest springs without getting wet, may occupy the meanest, most humble position without distress. He fills all Heaven and earth; and the more he gives to others, the more he has for himself.'"

CHAPTER 58

"...The Barrier Keeper Yin replied, 'This is because he guards the pure breath—it has nothing to do with wisdom, skill, determination, or courage. Sit down and I will tell you about it. All that have faces, forms, voices, colors—these are all mere things. How could one thing and another thing be far removed from each other? And how could any one of them be worth considering as a predecessor? They are forms, colors—nothing more. But things have their creation in what has no form, and their conclusion in what has no change. If a man can get hold of this and exhaust it fully, then how can things stand in his way? He may rest within the bounds that know no excess, hide within the borders that know no source, wander where the ten thousand things have their end and beginning, unify his nature, nourish his breath, unite his virtue, and thereby communicate with that which creates all things. A man like this guards what belongs to Heaven and keeps it whole. His spirit has no flaw, so how can things enter in and get at him?

"'When a drunken man falls from a carriage, though the carriage may be going very fast, he won't be killed. He has bones and joints the same as other men, and yet he is not injured as they would be, because his spirit is whole. He didn't know he was riding, and he doesn't know he has fallen out. Life and death, alarm and terror do not enter his breast, and so he can bang against things without fear of injury. If he can keep himself whole like this by means of wine, how much more can he keep himself whole by means of Heaven! The sage hides himself in Heaven—hence there is nothing that can do him harm.'"

CHAPTER 59

"Nieh Ch'üeh asked P'i-i about the Way. P'i-i said, 'Straighten up your body, unify your vision, and the harmony of Heaven will come to you. Call in your knowledge, unify your bearing, and the spirits will come to dwell with you. Virtue will be your beauty, the Way will be your home, and, stupid as a newborn calf, you will not try to find out the reason why.'"

BIBLIOGRAPHY

Fung Yu-lan. *Chuang-tzu: A New Selected Translation with an Exposition of the Philosophy of Kuo Hsiang*. Shanghai: The Commercial Press, 1931.

A. C. Graham. *Chuang-tzŭ: The Seven Inner Chapters and other writings from the book Chuang-tzŭ*. Boston: Allen & Unwin, 1981.

Sam Hamill and J. P. Seaton. *The Essential Chuang Tzu*. Boston: Shambhala, 1998.

David Hinton. *Chuang Tzu: The Inner Chapters*. Washington, D.C.: Counterpoint, 1997.

Byron Katie, with Stephen Mitchell. *A Thousand Names for Joy*. New York: Harmony Books, 2007.

Ku Hungming. "Central Harmony." In *The Wisdom of Confucius*, edited by Lin Yutang. New York: Modern Library, 1938.

Victor H. Mair. *Wandering on the Way: Early Taoist Tales and Parables of Chuang Tzu*. New York: Bantam, 1994.

Thomas Merton. *The Way of Chuang Tzu*. New York: New Directions, 1965.

Martin Palmer, with Elizabeth Breuilly. *The Book of Chuang Tzu*. New York: Viking Penguin, 1996.

Octavio Paz. *Chuang-Tzu*. Madrid: Ediciones Siruela, 1998.

Andrew Plaks. *Ta Hsüeh and Chung Yung*. New York: Penguin, 2003.

Ezra Pound. *The Unwobbling Pivot & The Great Digest*. New York: New Directions, 1951.

Harold D. Roth. ed. *A Companion to Angus C. Graham's* Chuang Tzu. Honolulu: University of Hawai'i Press, 2003.

Burton Watson. *The Complete Works of Chuang Tzu*. New York: Columbia University Press, 1968.

Richard Wilhelm. *Dschuang Dsi: Das Wahre Buch vom Südlichen Blütenland*. Jena: Diederichs, 1912.

ACKNOWLEDGMENTS

After I had finished a draft of the sixty-four adaptations, and thought that I was pretty much done except for the Foreword and Notes, my old friend and agent Michael Katz said, "Why not open the book completely and follow the thread of the Tao right into the present day?" Hence the Commentaries. Thank you, Michael, once again.

Ann Godoff, my editor and publisher, couldn't have been more supportive, passionate, or astute. There is no way to express my gratitude.

I am also grateful to James Autry, Chana Bloch, Rachel Boughton, Richard Lawrence Cohen, Thomas Farber, Pico Iyer, Erica Jong, Jon Kabat-Zinn, and Christie McDonald for their many helpful suggestions.

And thank you, dearest Katie, for the No to "Will you still need me?" and the Yes to "Will you still feed me?" (in so many unfathomable ways).